MICHAEL BARRY'S
Old English Recipes

MICHAEL BARRY'S
Old English Recipes
Classic Recipes from English Country Houses

 JARROLD PUBLISHING

This edition published by Jarrold Publishing, Norwich,
in association with SAWD Books, an imprint of SAWD Publications.
Placketts Hole, Bicknor, Sittingbourne, Kent ME9 8BA
in partnership with
The Arts and Libraries Department, Kent Country Council,
County Hall, Maidstone, Kent ME14 1XQ.

Originally published as Michael Barry's *Great House Cookery*
First published in hardback 1992.
Reprinted in paperback 1993.
This edition 1995

Design: Rachel Griffin
Photography: Tony Robins
Art Director of Photography: Caroline Greville-Morris
Stylist: Abi Manox
Home Economist: Susie Magasina
Flowers: Persephone Chetwynd
Index: Val Dudley

British Library Cataloguing-in-Publication Data
A catalogue record for this book is available from the British Library.

ISBN 0-7117-0811-8

Printed in Great Britain.

Contents

INTRODUCTION

For a cook who also by chance happens to be a historian, writing and researching this book has been an extraordinary pleasure. Recent years have seen a number of extremely scholarly as well as vivid publications on our cooking heritage. People like the late Elizabeth David, Jane Grigson and Michael Smith rediscovered our culinary heritage and the reasons we had to be proud of it, after many decades of neglect and contempt. They also unearthed a fascinating chain of cookery books stretching back into medieval times. By the 18th century this trend to produce such books in Britain had reached quite bestseller like proportions, Mrs Beeton was the heir to a great tradition, not the beginning of one.

But parallel to the published works of Hannah Glasse, John Farley and Eliza Acton, a second more private tradition of recipe collection was in operation. I first discovered it myself almost by accident at a sale of books owned by the late Raymond Postgate who founded the Good Food Guide. The sale included a collection of manuscript books from the 17th century onwards, most written in one or at most two hands, and each being a personal collection of recipes that had either caught a fancy or been donated by a friend or relative. Although I was much taken with one of these books, the prices were at that time, beyond my reach. So my excitement was doubled when the opportunity arose to base a book on a whole collection of such manuscripts and household and family recipe books.

The Centre for Kentish Studies' collection ranged from individual pieces of paper, including the proverbial back of an 18th century envelope, to fully bound and carefully annotated books of recipes, herbal receipts, nostrums and chemical formulae for producing everything from dinner to a cure for a sick horse. Their age ranged from the beginning of the 17th century, when the Stuarts were newly on the throne of England, through to the middle of the 19th century, when Victoria had recently begun her reign. They were all in handwriting, though some of them were written into diaries and notebooks with printed advice and information of their own. There were thousands of recipes and directions reflecting a world where there were no convenience foods unless you had made them yourself some time before. A time where there were no chemists, pharmacists or vets and few doctors, never mind supermarkets or freezers or food processors. In many ways not a time to envy in simple nostalgia. Even for the rich and prosperous it was a hard life, and fraught always with the threat of ill health or accident, shortage or spoilage, with few outside resources except what you and your family could provide or had put by.

But the papers I read also showed something else. Throughout that 250 years, the pleasures that plenty had occasionally provided had been greatly enjoyed. The short seasons of fruit and other produce had been valued for their very brevity. And people had *known* the produce - had cooked it skilfully and eaten well. This book is a distillation of some of the more accessible of these recipes that made that possible.

For most of us now that foods are plentifully and continuously available, constraint is often the watchword in our diet, less fat , less sugar, less salt. It seems clear from the archives that our forefathers knew no such restraints, so in addition to the original recipes, and a brief commentary on them, I have added a modern version. I have tried, without changing the intentions or flavour of the original, to make the recipes cookable in our modern idiom holding onto the essence of the dish.

I hope also to have conveyed some of the intense excitement. The excitement at unfolding a piece of paper to trace the writing and through it the life and mind and skills of a writer more than 300 years ago. When I was a history student, real documents like these were far too good for grubby-fingered undergraduates and so I enjoyed a new sense of contact and shared experience, when sifting through the original documents which remains with me still when I read even a transcription of one of the recipes.

I have added a brief outline of the families and their houses from which these books and collections came. Visiting some of them, often dramatically changed in their usage from the family homes of past centuries, added another dimension to this study. But there were extraordinary moments of discovery too. A recipe donor known as Cosen Dering, perhaps a term of affection, suddenly came to life in the Kent County Council offices. Whilst I was waiting for a meeting, a portrait on the wall turned out to be that of a Mary Dering, a surname, not an early spelling of a term of affection. She was a cousin of one of the recipe collectors, a noted collector in her own right.

I would like to pay tribute to the collectors, like the earliest one, Lady Rachel Fane, who turns out to have been making meringues nearly a hundred years before the French deigned to invent them, through some of the anonymous writers and cooks to the most contemporary, Delelah Tyler innocently copying one of Hannah Glasse's recipes into her own manuscript book. They have all left us a great legacy, an understanding of good food, a pleasure in its preparation and cooking, and a delight in the company with whom they shared it. I have tried to do justice to their skills, knowledge and enthusiasm, where I have fallen short it is through my own deficiencies, where I have succeeded it is to their credit.

However, none of this would have seen the light of day but for the commitment, enthusiasm and hard work of Susannah Wainman, my publisher, the skill and good humour of Alison Revell, who transcribed the original manuscript recipes and Tricia Rowsby and the staff of the Kent County Council Arts and Libraries Department, who were always patient and forever helpful guiding my inexperience through their treasure house. A mention also of Tony Robins, whose photographs capture so precisely the texture of the food and the atmosphere of the houses in which it was cooked and eaten, and Rachel Griffin, who has laid the book out in such a way that the old and the new live happily side by side.

Lastly, if you were to cook any of the modern versions of the recipes from the book, their hope of success is underwritten by the skills of Ray Bukht who tested and amended them with a craft and insight contributed by many years as a leading home economist. We all hope you will enjoy sharing the lives and dishes of our predecessors.

Michael Barry,
Canterbury 1992.

Order of Service

The layout of each season is with recipes in roughly the order in which we would eat them today with preserves coming at the end of each season. But until the middle of the 18th century food in Britain was normally eaten in a kind of sitting buffet, the French style of presentation as it was known. In domestic circumstances all the dishes were placed on the table at the same time and people helped themselves in the patterns they chose. On high days and holidays a series of courses were served but each of these would consist of up to 20 different dishes served at the same time. In poorer families, of course, the number of dishes was often drastically reduced to a single pot, but where the opportunity afforded, multiple choice was the order of the day.

This changed quite dramatically towards the end of the 18th century with the introduction of what was known as the Russian service, in the style in which we know it today. Individual dishes and their immediate accompaniments were then served in a series of courses one after the other, each being cleared away before the next one arrived. This was still a much more large-scale affair than we are used to now, with 8 or 9 courses being the norm and indeed 5 or 6 being unexceptional in middle class families until after the end of the First World War. That shouldn't stop you using the soups or lighter dishes as a starter, the main courses which are self evident, and the puddings which then as now were so enormously popular as a sweet course, to provide the three course meal that is our standard. Some of the dishes though, not least because of their origins, lend themselves to buffets and you can capture something of the flavour of a late Renaissance banquet by using them in that way.

Until the end of the 19th century the Spring months in Britain - March, April and May - were for the most part, a time of severe shortages in the kitchen. With our Northern European climate not a great deal had grown sufficiently to be harvested by the end of May and from March onwards the stores and supplies from last summer's harvests didn't amount to much.

The vast majority of the animals had to be slaughtered in the winter because of the shortage of fodder. However our ancestors were very sophisticated and able in the way of preserving foods, but even this meant that supplies were at their shortest in the Spring. It's probably this deprivation that made May so welcome. It was the beginning of the real growing season and summer's plenty to come, though, of course for most of the people writing the recipes in this book, the shortages were cushioned by wealth. Despite all of this, in Spring there was usually Easter to look forward to, a time of feasting and celebrating the end of the Lenten fast.

Spring was also a time of "clearing the blood", an old fashioned interpretation of the benefits that actually do accrue when you first come upon green vegetables after a long period on preserved and salted foods. One of the more unexpected aspects of this was, and in some country parts still is, the widespread consumption of nettles and other wild herbs. Indeed nettles were so prolific a grower early in Spring that in the 18th century they were widely cultivated as a first crop vegetable in many gardens. They still make a delicious soup without a trace of a sting once they're cooked. But although there are no nettle dishes here, this section does include a range of interesting and delicious foods, often using the store cupboard ingredients that could be kept most easily, and used until the fresh foods of Summer arrived.

Observations on March, 1765.

Full Moon the 7th Day, at 1 in the Afternoon.
Last Quarter the 14th Day, at 10 in the Morning.
New Moon the 21st Day, at 1 in the Afternoon.
First Quarter the 29th Day, at 3 in the Afternoon.

All Works in the Garden directed to be done last Month, must be finished in this : All Sorts of Grafting may be done this Month : Prune Nectarines, Peaches and Apricots. Set Slips of Sage, Rosemary, Lavender, Thyme, &c.

Continue to set Willows and other Aquaticks.

Spring Quarter begins on the 20th Day of March, at 8 in the Morning.

Sow Pease, Oats and Barley, and also all Sorts of Grass Seeds.

Purge and let Blood : Eat no gross Meats.

A 4

Observations on April, 1765.

Full Moon the 6th Day, at 1 in the Morning.
Last Quarter the 12th Day, at 4 in the Afternoon.
New Moon the 20th Day, at 4 in the Morning.
First Quarter the 28th Day, at 8 in the Morning.

With the Farmer and Gardener this is the busiest Month in the whole Year ; for now whatsoever you have a mind to plant or sow, the Earth is fit to receive. Hough your French-Beans, plant Asparagus, separate the Layers of Artichokes, and plant three of them in one Hole. Plant Garden Beans, Rouncival and other large Pease to succeed other Crops. Plant Slips of Sage, Rue, Rosemary, Lavender, &c. Sow all Sorts of Sallad Herbs, and Spinage in moist Places for the last Time. Sow Turnips, and all Sorts of Cabbage-Lettuce, and transplant Cos and Silesia Letuces which were sown last Month. It is now a good Time to bleed and take Physick ; abstain from much Wine, or other strong Liquors ; they will cause a Ferment in your Blood, and ruin your Constitution.

A 5

Observations on May, 1765.

Full Moon the 5th Day, at 10 in the Morning.
Last Quarter the 11th Day, at Midnight.
New Moon the 19th Day, at 8 in the Afternoon.
First Quarter the 27th Day, at 10 at Night.

Sow Cucumbers in the natural Ground, as also Purslane and Cabbages ; sow Pease and Beans in a moist Soil for a latter Crop ; plant Kidney-Beans for a second Crop, and transplant Sellery into Drills ; hough your Winter Crop of Carrots, Beans, Onions, &c. which will save much Labour the succeeding Months. Sow Turnips, and if Rain comes soon after it will very much encourage the Plant. Sow Buck-Wheat and latter Pease. Weed young Quicksets and Ivy ; fallow your Ground ; look well to your Sheep, if the Weather proves wet, for fear of a Rot. The Blood and Humours being now in Motion, we must be careful to avoid eating Salt, strong or stale Meats ; fat People must avoid Excess of Liquors of any Kind.

spring

Bak'd Herrings

HUSSEY FAMILY, SCOTNEY CASTLE, EARLY 19TH CENTURY

The last line of this recipe in the original is perhaps the most extraordinary of what is otherwise an early version of soused herrings. The idea that they should cook for two nights is entirely based on the kind of ancient huge kitchen range that a great house like the one in Scotney Castle would have had, and which even a large modern Aga only barely represents. There would have been a series of ovens, at least one of which would have been of so gentle a temperature that food could be cooked in it over a period of 24 to 48 hours at the lowest possible simmer. It's simply not reproducible these days. My method produces delicious baked herrings and if you do have an Aga with four ovens, the slowest one, usually called the plate warmer, will cook this overnight, but one night only I'm afraid.

INGREDIENTS

4 herrings

½ pint each cider vinegar and boiled water

4 bay leaves

1 dessertspoon salt

1 teaspoon peppercorns

1 blade of mace

some toothpicks

METHOD

Cut the heads off the herrings, and if they are not already gutted, gut them. Then place with the opening down on a chopping board or work surface. Run your fingers down the backbone of the herring, pressing down very firmly along both sides of the fins from the top to the tail. Turn over, and you'll find that the whole of the backbone will pull out, taking with it almost all the fine ribs, leaving you with a kipper shaped herring. Roll them up from the head end to the tail, and skewer with a toothpick. Place them in a baking tin or casserole into which they just fit, and cover them with the vinegar and water, adding the bay leaves, salt, peppercorns and mace. Cover them with foil or butterpaper and put in a low oven, Gas Mark 1, 125°C, 250-275°F (or the lowest oven of an Aga), for up to 6 hours. Allow to cool before you eat them.

BAK'D HERRINGS
Gut and clean your Herring well, take out the Bone and role them up double and skewer them put them in a deep Pan cover them with half Vinegar and half water ad to it a handfull of Bay leaves Salt pepper and mace put them in a cool oven two night will bake them.

Flounders

Flounders, in modern Britain, don't have much of a reputation. They're a kind of estuarine plaice that one recipe book I know suggests are ideal for cats. When this recipe was written, though, at the turn of the 18th century, flounders meant a range of flat fish including, probably, plaice and witch soles, which even today are still known in parts of the East Coast as 'pale flounders'. Certainly in America, where so many of our recipes and linguistic traditions emigrated in the 18th century, flounder still means a number of different flat fish caught at different times of year. They closely resemble our plaice and lemon or witch soles.

The method used to cook them seems quite ferocious compared to modern ways of dealing with fish, as it requires both frying and 'stewing'. What's more, the recipe comes from a date when oysters were a food of the poor and therefore often used just to enrich sauces. The method however, when moderated by one or two modern techniques, produces a robust sauce that goes with the comparatively mild flavour of plaice, probably our best representative of the flounder clan these days.

INGREDIENTS

4 x 6 - 8 ozs plaice fillets

1 tablespoon each of oil and butter

1/2 pint water

1 tablespoon white wine vinegar

6 oysters, or the trimmings for the plaice, bones and head

2 tinned anchovy fillets

1 tablespoon each celery leaf, fennel leaf, and parsley, chopped

1 teaspoon thyme, chopped ,1/2 teaspoon powdered mace

Juice of half a lemon

2 ozs of butter, softened

4 slices of white bread, cut into triangles

METHOD

Put the water, vinegar, the oysters or plaice trimmings, the anchovy fillets, the celery leaf, fennel leaf, half the parsley, thyme, and the powdered mace, into a pan. Season with salt and pepper, bring to the boil and simmer for 30 minutes. Strain. Flour the plaice fillets and fry them lightly in the mixture of butter and oil until they are light brown. Place them in a baking dish in which they will lie flat, pour the strained liquid over them and bake in a medium oven, Gas Mark 4, 180°C, 350°F, for 15 minutes. Carefully lift the fish onto a serving dish, and into the remaining liquid, with a whisk, beat the butter. Whisk it, making a light sauce, without allowing the butter to go oily. Add the lemon juice, pour over the fish, and sprinkle with the remaining parsley. While the fish is baking, fry the bread till crisp, or brush with a little oil and bake in the oven till crisp. Arrange these 'sippets' around the fish in an attractive pattern and serve.

Carrot Soup

Carrot soup as eaten by the Hussey family in their house in the ruins of Scotney Castle was a substantial affair. The recipe in its original form was certainly enough to feed the family and servants' hall. This sort of vegetable soup was made in the Spring from stored vegetables kept in clamps or heavily earthed up as the celery would have been to protect it from frost. It's not at all a rustic vegetable soup, with the fine finishing and thickening of eggs and cream. It may be that this is the result of a French influence, owing to the very cosmopolitan acquaintance of the Hussey family: the archives contain a number of books simply full of their contacts and addresses. But it may also be an indication of the considerable sophistication of English cookery at the time. It was regarded by many, including our continental cousins, as the equal of any in Europe. In the original, and in my modern version, mutton or lamb is used as the flavouring for the stock.If you fancy a lighter soup, substitute chicken stock in its place.

INGREDIENTS

1 lb scrag end of neck of lamb

2 pints of water

1 bay leaf

1 teaspoon of chopped thyme

1½ lb onions, with the inner skin carefully washed; the rest finely chopped

1 lb carrots, peeled and cut in half lengthwise

½ head of celery, diced

1 tablespoon of parsley, with the heads finely chopped and the stalks kept separate

1 egg

4 tablespoons cream

METHOD

Cut the lamb into inch sized cubes and place it in a pan with the water. Bring it to the boil and skim. Simmer for 1½ to 2 hours with the bayleaf, thyme and inner skins of the onions. Strain the stock and place it in a bowl with some ice cubes. This will cause the fat to go solid and make it easy to remove with a slotted spoon. Place the clear stock back in a saucepan. (If using chicken stock, begin the recipe here.) Add the celery, onions, carrots, parsley stalks, and a teaspoon of salt, and simmer until the vegetables are soft. Remove the carrots, and a couple of ladlefuls of stock to a blender or processor and purée till smooth. Beat the egg with the cream, mix with the carrot mixture, and pour back into the soup. Reheat carefully, not allowing it to boil but allowing the cream and eggs to thicken. The chopped parsley can be sprinkled on the top as a garnish.

CARROT SOUPS
Take the scrag end of A neck of mutton 3 Quarts of Water stew it Over A slow fire six hours put five Large Onions 4 Large Carrots One Large head of Salary A few sweet hearbs pepper and salt strain it of somm of all the fat thicken it with two Eggs ad to it One small cup full of cream rub two Carrots through A seave to give it A collour.

Turkish Cubobb

MARSHAM FAMILY, CUXTON, LATE 17TH CENTURY

A taste for exotic food certainly seems to have existed in Britain long before the advent of Chinese take-aways and kebab houses. This recipe comes from the Marsham family who lived at Cuxton on the banks of the Medway in the 16th, 17th and early 18th centuries before they moved to Maidstone. It may well be that the Medway, from Elizabeth I's time a centre for ships, shipping and international trade brought up the recipe from Turkey - at the time a major power in the Mediterranean. Dating from the late 1600s, it's remarkable how little this dish has changed in its country of origin, or in the restaurants in which we now enjoy its cousins all over Britain. A dish of white rice with a crisp cucumber and tomato salad go particularly well with this dish.

INGREDIENTS

2 lbs neck fillet or leg of lamb, boned

5 onions, medium size, peeled

1 tablespoon each marjoram and savory, finely chopped

4 tablespoons parsley, finely chopped

Salt and Pepper

Juice of 1 lemon

2 further lemons cut into quarters

1 tablespoon of butter

METHOD

Cut the meat into one inch cubes. Pour half the lemon juice over the meat, season and turn in the herbs, making sure as much of them as possible stick to the meat. Allow to marinate for between 2 to 12 hours. Blanch the onions in boiling water for 3 minutes and cut them carefully in half lengthwise. Take eight skewers, separate the onion rings allowing a thickness of two or three rings together. Skewer a section of onion, then a piece of meat, then a section of onion, and so on, until you have used up all the meat and onions in equal quantities, on the skewers. Pack them quite closely together at the sharp end, making sure that the onion does not fully enclose the meat. Heat a grill very hot, and grill for 5 minutes a side. The onions will crisp in places but the meat should be brown on the outside and still moist in the centre. Place on a serving dish. Melt the butter and add the remaining lemon juice to pour over the kebabs. Serve with the lemon quarters.

*RICH GOSLINGS TURKISH DISH
CALLED A CUBOBB*
*Take a line or nick of mutten cut it in 10 peeces
then take 10 very large onions boyle them a little to make them hange on the spitt take time
margerum savery & a great deale of parsly
shreed the earbs & clipe the meat & onions in
bitts to make the earbs stick, season them well
with peper & salt & spitt an onion between every
peece of meat. When rosted put them all together into a dish for sause put butter & vinigar.
Sarve it up with lemon.*

A Page Turning over a leaf. JB.

*What does the Wind do in Spring.
It turns a New Leaf –*

Recipe for making a *Salad*

BY THE REVEREND SYDNEY SMITH, STANHOPE FAMILY, CHEVENING, 1840S

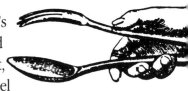

Sydney Smith was a famous 19th century Divine, a Canon of St. Paul's renowned for his love of the good things in life, his generous spirit, and the good company he provided. He was everybody's favourite dinner guest, being able, so history recounts, to make anyone with whom he spoke feel interesting. Although his own parish was in the West Country, his duties at St. Paul's brought him to London and the Home Counties for three months of the year where he took full opportunity to visit friends and acquaintances. He seems to have been a frequent guest of the Stanhopes, both at their house in Chevening and the other residences they had in and around the Capital. He left them this marvellous recipe in verse for a salad. In fact the recipe isn't for the salad itself, but a salad dressing, similar to the salad creams that were common in 18th and 19th century English cooking, before the noxious bottled version took over. It's marvellous served with hard boiled eggs, like a mayonnaise, or with a salad made with equal quantities of chopped celery and apple and a half portion of chopped walnuts. You could add some diced chicken to this to make a form of early Waldorf Salad. It's also delicious with cold poached salmon, eaten with cucumber salad, and hot, new potatoes.

INGREDIENTS

¼ lb peeled potatoes

½ teaspoon English mustard, made up

½ teaspoon salt

3 tablespoons virgin olive oil

2 tablespoons cider or white wine vinegar, or lemon juice

2 hard boiled eggs

1 slice of Spanish onion

1 teaspoon anchovy sauce or anchovy essence

4 tablespoons milk

This recipe can't be made in a liquidiser or processor as the potatoes turn to glue, so a sieve or a mouli legumes is ideal.

METHOD

Steam the potatoes until thoroughly soft and pass through a sieve or mouli legumes or mash until thoroughly smooth. Stir in the milk, mustard and salt. Mix the oil and vinegar together and pour these in, stirring till fully incorporated. Sieve or thoroughly mash the yolks of the hard boiled eggs and stir those in. Rub the bowl in which you are going to keep the dressing with the sliced onion so that it smears, but add no substantial part of the onion itself. Pour the dressing in and stir it well. Add the teaspoon of anchovy sauce and mix thoroughly. Allow to amalgamate its flavours for an hour or two in the fridge before using.

RECEIPT FOR MAKING A SALAD (DRESSING)
by the
Revd. Sydney Smith

Two large Potatoes passed thro' Kitchen seive Unwonted softness to the Salad give, Of ardent mustard add a single spoon, Distrust the condiment which bites too soon; But deem it not, thou man of herbs, a fault To add a double quantity of salt; Three times the spoon with oil of Lucca crown; And once with Vinegar procured from town; True flavour needs it and your Poet begs, The pounded yellow of two well boiled eggs; Let onion atoms lurk within the bowl, And scarce suspected animate the whole; And lastly on the flavoured compound toss, A magic teaspoon of Anchovy Sauce; Then - though green turtle fail, tho' Venison's tough, And ham & turkey are not boiled enough, Serenely full, the Epicure may say - Fate cannot harm me - I have dined today!

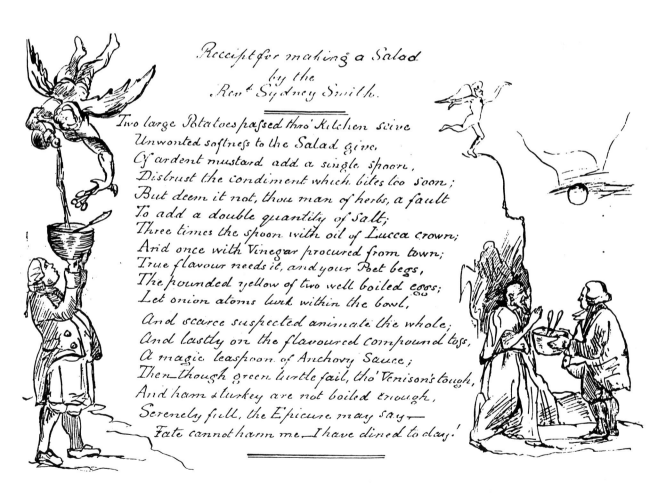

Fricandello's

HUSSEY FAMILY, SCOTNEY CASTLE, EARLY 19TH CENTURY

Fricandello's and other similar names are used all over Northern Europe to describe meatballs, or rissoles as we would call them now. In Britain since the War they've been rather poorly regarded because they were often made from leftover ingredients but this dish clearly was designed to make the most of good-quality ingredients. It's an early 18th-century recipe and makes a delicious main course for six which goes very well with some spinach and baked potatoes. I've used turkey very successfully in this recipe, replacing veal; it's easier to come by and, for many people, more comfortable to eat in the light of some of the ways veal is currently raised.

INGREDIENTS

1 ½ lbs turkey fillet or boneless veal, cut into cubes

2 tablespoons sunflower or olive oil

6 ozs white breadcrumbs

½ teaspoon ground nutmeg

2 tablespoons parsley, chopped

2 eggs

1 cup of water

Juice of half a lemon

1 dessertspoon cornflour, slaked in 2 tablespoons of water

METHOD

Mince the veal or turkey in a food processor or a conventional mincer. Add the oil and the breadcrumbs, and season with salt and pepper and the nutmeg. Add the parsley and knead together with the two eggs (if the eggs are very large you may need only one egg and an egg yolk). Separate into 24 pieces, and roll each into a slightly elongated ball shape. Fry them in a non-stick or well seasoned pan in one layer in a tablespoon or two of oil for 15 minutes until well browned but not dry. Remove the fricandello's to a serving dish and keep warm. Add the water into the frying pan, bring to the boil and stir in the lemon juice and the slaked cornflour. Allow this gravy to thicken and then pour over the fricandello's before serving.

FRICANDELLO'S
Put one pound a half of lean veal fine in a mortar, put to it half a pound of veal, Beef or Mutton fat, & the crumb of a stale french roll grated, season these ingredients with a little salt pepper & nutmeg & a little parsley shred fine. make them up into short thick sausages with the yolk of 2 Eggs and fry them in butter of a light brown, then stir them about a quarter of an hour, thicken the gravy with flour & butter & squeeze in some lemon juice just before you serve it up.

Frigasey of Rabbetts

MARSHAM FAMILY, WHORNES PLACE, 17TH-18TH CENTURY

The style and arbitrariness of the spelling for this recipe suggest that it is one of the earlier ones collected by the Marsham family at Cuxton near Rochester. In those days in Britain, as indeed in France today, rabbits were regarded as a delicacy. It uses claret, which was practically a staple in rich English households of the time - white wine, although still produced occasionally domestically, wasn't much imported or drunk. To our tastes, red wine and rabbit are not the most comfortable of combinations and I think we might prefer to try white wine, cider, or apple juice - I think the last benefits the dish by giving it a hint of sweetness. This dish should be served onto warm plates with mashed potatoes, carrots and broccoli.

INGREDIENTS

2 lb rabbit pieces

Bouquet garni made of a sprig of thyme, piece of celery leaf, large sprig of parsley and a couple of bay leaves, tied together

1/2 teaspoon each of ground nutmeg and black pepper

1 tablespoon anchovy sauce or anchovy essence

1/2 pint apple juice, dry cider or white wine

1 onion, sliced in rings

Blade of mace

2 tablespoons lemon juice

4 egg yolks, beaten

4 ozs butter

METHOD

Rub the rabbit pieces with the anchovy essence and sprinkle them with the nutmeg and pepper. Melt half the butter and fry the rabbit pieces in it until lightly browned. Fry the onion with the rabbit for one minute. Add the apple juice, cider or wine, the lemon juice and the blade of mace and simmer for 25 minutes until the rabbit is cooked. Add the remaining butter to the pan, and stir in the egg yolks away from the heat. The sauce will thicken almost immediately.

HOW TO MAKE A FRIGASEY OF RABBETTS
Take a Couple of Rabbetts & cut them in pieces and season them with sweete herbs nutmeg pepper anchovis & fry them in butter then take halfe a pynt of Clarrett some anchovis and onion mace and Leamon and boyle them together than take them off, and putt 4 yolkes of eggs and some butter then put altogether in the pann taking it of the fire and shake it soundly to keepe it from Curdling for the heat of the pan and Lyquor will be hott enough to make it. Serve it up with Leamon.

Scotch Collops

TWISDEN FAMILY, BRADBOURNE PARK, 1675-1750

By the time Mrs Beeton came to write about them, Scotch Collops were always made from cooked veal cut into slices - it was a way of using up leftovers - but the recipes of an earlier date often begin with the raw meat itself. There are, in the Archives, many versions of Scotch Collops and this is perhaps one of the earliest, from "Dyvers Receipts in Physicke and Cookery by a discrete oulde and maiden gentlewoman" of the Twisden family who lived at Bradbourne near East Malling. The recipe is quite complicated but, because of the addition of the forcemeat balls (which contain no meat), it's quite a generous meal for six people. Although this would not have been included in the 18th century, I think that these Collops go extremely well with the broad flat pasta called Tagliatelli, perhaps with a salad to follow.

INGREDIENTS

1 1/2 lbs veal or turkey escalopes in 12 evenly sliced pieces

1/2 teaspoon each of ground cloves, mace, nutmeg and pepper

2 ozs fresh white breadcrumbs

1/2 pint well flavoured chicken or beef stock

Half an onion, finely chopped

1 anchovy fillet (optional)   2 tablespoons butter

FORCEMEAT BALLS: 6 ozs white breadcrumbs

Half an onion, finely chopped

4 ozs button mushrooms, finely chopped

2 tablespoons milk

1 egg

2 tablespoons parsley, finely chopped , 1 teaspoon each thyme and marjoram, chopped

SAUCE: 2 egg yolks, well beaten

1 tablespoon butter

1 tablespoon cornflour, slaked in 4 tablespoons of water

TO SERVE:

Fried or baked bread triangles and lemon quarters

METHOD

With a heavy knife blade or meat hammer, gently flatten the escalopes. Season with the cloves, mace, nutmeg and pepper, and leave aside. In a bowl, mix the 6 ozs breadcrumbs, half the onion, the button mushrooms, the parsley, the thyme and marjoram with the two tablespoons of milk and the egg to make a firm mixture. Divide into twelve portions and roll into neat balls. Sprinkle the escalopes with the remaining 2 ozs white breadcrumbs, pressing them in where possible. Melt 2 tablespoons of butter in a frying pan large enough to take all the escalopes at one time in one layer, and fry over a brisk heat until brown. Add the stock, the other half of the onion and the anchovy fillet if you are using it. Add the forcemeat balls and simmer for 10 minutes, turning both the meat and the balls halfway. With a slotted spoon, remove the meat to a serving dish, and surround it with the forcemeat balls. Add the butter and the slaked cornflour to the sauce and stir. Take off the heat, add the two egg yolks, and mix well. Re-heat until the sauce is thickened, and pour over the veal and forcemeat balls. Serve surrounded by the fried bread triangles and lemon quarters.

SCOTCH COLLOPS

Cutt the Leane off a Leg of veale into thine slices beatte it with the back off a knife Season itt with Cloves mace nuttmeg and peper a Little Gratted bread then Fry itt browne with butter then Cleane outt the pan and putt in a Ladle Full of strong broth halff a pint off whitte wine one anchove two shallots 20 Force meat balls half a pound of Fresh butter then Clap in your Collops and Lett it boyle up then beatte itt thick with the yealks off 2 or 3 eggs sarve it with sipits Garnish itt with Lemon and barberyes.

To Dress White Scotch collops
Do not dip them in Egg but fry them till they are tender but not brown, take your meat out of the pan and pour all out then put in your meat again as above, only you must put in sum cream —

TWISDEN FAMILY

The Twisden family was established for centuries at Royden Hall and then from the mid 17th century in addition at Bradbourne Park. This part of the line reached its high point in the following hundred years until family feuding and a series of childless heirs terminated it at the beginning of this century. The cookery book in the archives is a substantial volume, foolscap in shape. It was the work of "a discrete oulde and maiden gentlewoman". An, as yet, unidentified relative of Sir Thomas Twisden, it was written primarily from 1675 into the early 1700s, with some later additions in different hands up to around 1750.

Rice Pudding

HUSSEY FAMILY, SCOTNEY CASTLE, 18TH CENTURY

A very different style of rice pudding from the one we eat in Britain today. This recipe from the 18th century was collected by the Hussey family on the Kent/Sussex border and is nearer in many ways to a soufflé than the kind of rice pudding we are used to. The instructions don't say how you should cook it and it may well have been, in its original form, put in a fine linen cloth heavily buttered and floured, and then boiled. I think the modern version should undoubtedly be baked in a moderate oven, and this should be done in a bain marie or water jacket to create a gentle and moist heat.

INGREDIENTS

2 ozs ground rice

1 pint 'breakfast' or Channel Island milk

4 egg yolks

3 egg whites

4 ozs caster sugar

4 ozs butter

1 oz slivered almonds

1/2 teaspoon ground nutmeg

2 ozs mixed peel

METHOD

Stir the rice carefully into the milk until smooth and add the sugar. Bring it to the boil, stirring well. Simmer for one minute, add the butter, and allow to cool. When cool mix in the egg yolks. Beat the whites until firm and fold into the mixture, adding the almonds, nutmeg and mixed peel. Put in a buttered soufflé dish or pudding basin, and put this in a bain marie with at least an inch of water (a roasting dish will do fine) and bake in a preheated oven, Gas Mark 4, 180°C, 350°F, for 35 to 40 minutes until the pudding is set. If it starts to brown at the top, cover with a butter paper. This can be eaten hot with extra cream, or cold.

TO MAKE A RICE PUDDING
a quarter of a pound of Ground Rice boil it in a quart of New Milk & cool it. beat Nine Eggs Leave out 3 Whits half a pound of Sugar half a pound of Butter: 2 Ounces of Almonds & a Nutmeg as Much Citron as you please & Orange peel.

Orange Puddings

Orange Pudding

HUSSEY FAMILY, SCOTNEY CASTLE, 18TH & 19TH CENTURY

Until this century, oranges were one of the great luxuries of life in Britain. All through medieval times right up until the late 18th century oranges almost always meant Seville oranges, the kind we now use for marmalade and the occasional sauce with duck. The sweet kind came from China via Portugal and were, until recently, always very expensive. Puddings made with them were therefore a great treat. As both Sevilles and sweet oranges in those days were at their peak in the Spring (many varieties flower at the time the fruit's really ripe) and little else was fresh and available, everything conspired to make orange puddings a delight in the first part of the year. I have got four variations here, the first from the Hussey family in Scotney Castle, a rich family who could afford plenty of oranges for their puddings, and sophisticated enough to distinguish between Civil (Seville) and sweet oranges.

INGREDIENTS

3 oranges, (1 sweet and 2 Seville) or 3 oranges and the juice of a lemon

4 ozs white breadcrumbs

4 ozs orange juice or white wine

4 eggs, separated

4 ozs each butter and caster sugar

6 ozs shortcrust pastry

METHOD

Grate the rind of two oranges (if you've got Sevilles, one sweet and one bitter) and juice them all, adding the lemon juice if you have no bitter oranges. Mix the juice, the breadcrumbs, the grated rind, and the extra orange juice or white wine together and leave to soak. Melt the butter, add the caster sugar, and when it's melted take off the heat. Add the 4 egg yolks and mix everything into the breadcrumb mixture. Beat the whites until firm, and fold those in. Roll out the pastry and line an 8 inch tart tin. Pour the mixture into the tart tin and bake for 45 minutes to an hour in a pre-heated oven at Gas Mark 3, 170°C, 325°F.

> ### ORANGE PUDDING
> *Grate the thin yellow rind of two Oranges/one of them civil - the Juice of four - 5 ounces of grated crumbs of Bread - a large Wine Glass of White Wine made Hot pourd on the Bread to soak - the(n) mix the peels and Juice beat the Yolks of 4 Eggs the whites of two - add 6 ounces of melted Butter dº of white Sugar mix it altogether bake it near an Hour on a Dish with paste at the Bottom.*

An exceedingly nice boiled orange pudding

UNKNOWN, 1818

Another early 19th century recipe uses preserved orange in two forms, as marmalade and as orange flower water.

INGREDIENTS

½ lb white breadcrumbs

16 fl ozs milk

3 ozs butter

2 eggs, well beaten

2 ozs caster sugar

2 tablespoons orange marmalade

1 teaspoon orange flower water

SAUCE

2 tablespoons of butter

Juice of half a lemon

1 tablespoon caster sugar

1 tablespoon brandy (optional)

METHOD

Mix the breadcrumbs and milk together in a non stick saucepan and bring to the boil. When simmering, add the butter and stir till mixed. Let it cool and add the two eggs, and caster sugar. Carefully stir in the marmalade. Do not be tempted to use more, it will sink to the bottom. Add the orange flower water. Butter a 2 pint pudding basin and pour the mixture in. Cover with a piece of greaseproof paper with a pleat folded into it. Place it in a saucepan with boiling water halfway up and simmer with the lid on for an hour and a quarter. (It will cook in 30 to 40 minutes in a pressure cooker.)

FOR THE SAUCE: Melt a couple of tablespoons of butter, the juice of half a lemon, and stir in a tablespoon of caster sugar. Add, if you wish, a tablespoon of brandy.

Oringe Pudding

TWISDEN FAMILY, BRADBOURNE PARK, 1675-1750

From an earlier time, the end of the 17th century, comes this recipe. It uses candied orange and lemon peel, a favourite way of preserving the flavour of the fruits in those days. A very similar recipe, but lightened with almonds and breadcrumbs, was the origin of the Bakewell Tart or Bakewell Pudding which traditionally had candied orange and lemon peel or candied apricots as its base rather than the raspberry jam we have come to expect today. I'm including the recipe in its original form, without a modern version, because it's more a sweetmeat in the medieval and early Tudor style than a dish for modern tastes.

IT IS AS FOLLOWS TO MAKE AN ORINGE PUDING

Take ye yolks of 10 eggs & half a pound of melted Butter & half a pound of suger stir all these together then put a puff past att ye bottom of ye Dish then take a quarter of a pound of canded orange & Lemon pill & lay it at ye Bottom of ye Dish & Bake it when it is come out of ye oven some juice of Lemon will doe very well in it

Orange Custard

CHAMPNEYS FAMILY, LYMPNE, 1830S

The fourth of this selection of orange dishes comes from the 1830s, from the Champneys family who lived at Lympne. By this time oranges were more widely available and the quantities used are therefore much greater. This is really a kind of orange fool that's as attractive to look at as to eat, if served chilled in large wine glasses.

INGREDIENTS

1 pint orange juice, Seville if possible, if not, ^{1}/3 grapefruit, ^{2}/3 orange juice

6 egg yolks

4 ozs caster sugar

1 tablespoon butter

Candied orange peel segments for decoration

METHOD

Beat the yolks of 6 eggs thoroughly and mix them with the juice. Sieve them into a non stick saucepan. Add the caster sugar and bring *very gently* up to a heat which melts the sugar but does not boil the mixture. Stir it continuously until it is as thick as double cream. When it reaches this point, stir in the butter, take off the heat and allow to cool a little before pouring into serving glasses. Chill in the fridge overnight, and decorate with candied orange peel segments before serving.

> *TO MAKE AN ORANGE CUSTARD*
> *Take a Pint of the Juice of Seville Oranges and put to it the Yolks of six new lay'd eggs very well beaten, steep the Peel of 2 of the Oranges in the Juice whilst you beat the Eggs, then mix them together & run them through a fine sieve sweeten it to your taste & set it on a clear fire, not too quick keep it continually stirring till it is as thick as a Custard, when it begins to simmer put a piece of Butter in the bigness of a Walnut.*

A Magic Square.

11	24	7	20	3
4	12	25	8	16
17	5	13	21	9
10	18	1	14	22
23	6	19	2	15

Gooseberry Cream

TWISDEN FAMILY, BRADBOURNE PARK, 1675-1750

This recipe from the Twisden family's 'discrete oulde and maiden gentlewoman' is a general purpose recipe for making fruit fools - mixtures of sweetened fruit and whipped cream or thick cream-based custard. These were extremely popular desserts from the 17th century onwards and were adjusted to suit the season and the available fruit. Gooseberry Fool, the leading star in this group, is as much a favourite today as it was then.

The white gooseberries referred to in the text, by the way, were eating gooseberries; the distinction between eating and cooking gooseberries is not so obvious these days, when cross breeding has produced fruit that serves both purposes.

INGREDIENTS

1/2 pint double cream

4 ozs caster sugar

1 teaspoon orange flower water

1 lb gooseberries, topped and tailed

ALTERNATIVE INGREDIENTS IN PLACE OF GOOSEBERRIES

1 lb cooking apples, peeled and cored

1 tablespoon water

METHOD

Bring the double cream to the boil, simmer one minute and allow it to cool. Put the orange flower water, sugar and gooseberries together and simmer very gently until the gooseberries soften. If you like a very smooth fool, process them, but if you like some texture mash them gently; cool and add to the double cream. Pour into pretty serving dishes and allow to set.

METHOD FOR APPLE ALTERNATIVE:

Bring the double cream to the boil, simmer one minute and allow it to cool as before. Cook 3/4 lb of the apples with the caster sugar, the orange flower water and a tablespoon of plain water, until soft. Process them to a fine purée. Slice the remaining 1/4 lb apples thinly, add to the puree and cook for another five minutes so that they retain some texture. Beat into the cream and allow to cool before serving.

GOOSEBERRY CREAM

Boyl your cream very well then season it with suggar and orange flower water, and strain as much scalded Gooseberries as you please stir it well and serve it cold thus you may serve white Gooseberries but they must not be scalded only plumpt and strain'd - thus you may make codling cream stir in some and slice in other, so you may green apricocks.

Gooseberry Jam

HUSSEY FAMILY, SCOTNEY CASTLE, EARLY 19TH CENTURY

Gooseberries have long been the British fruit. The Germans have used them only occasionally and the French, despite much urging, have steadfastly refused even to give them a name of their own, using the same word as that for redcurrant. This is possibly because the gooseberries they were most familiar with, in the 18th and 19th centuries, were red gooseberries. They are the ingredients for this jam and it is still possible, sometimes, to find red gooseberries on sale. If you grow your own, the variety Whinhams Industry produces the red berries needed. It's an early 19th century jam and is really more of a conserve - a very thick preserve as good to eat with a spoon as to spread on bread.

Cherries, stoned, and damsons likewise make similar jams. It's easiest to stone the fruit, I find, after it's been cooked when most of the stones float to the surface.

INGREDIENTS

1 lb red (or ordinary) goose-berries, topped, tailed and sliced in half

4 ozs redcurrants

1/2 lb preserving sugar

METHOD

Liquidise the redcurrants and strain the juice off - it should produce about four tablespoons. Cook the gooseberries in the redcurrant juice until thoroughly softened. Add the sugar and allow to dissolve off the heat. Stir thoroughly and cook gently again until the jam sets when a drop or two is placed on a refrigerated saucer. Bottle it in wide topped sterilised jars that you can get the preserve out of easily.

GOOSEBERRY JAM

To a pound of red Gooseberries cut in halves put four spoonfulls of red Currant juice and half a Pound of Sugar - boil it till stiff - Cherry and Damson cheese done the same to Cherry add the Kernels not so much Sugar quite

Births —— Marriages —— Deaths
Hatch —— Match —— Despatch

Spinach Tart

TWISDEN FAMILY, BRADBOURNE PARK, 1675-1750

Spinach tarts in the 17th century, when this particular one was enjoyed at Bradbourne Park by the Twisden family, were sweet not savoury affairs. Spinach was one of the first green vegetables that was harvestable in the late spring after the long winter of preserved foods; in all sorts of recipes, whether as a sauce for poultry or on its own, it often had sugar or dried fruit added to it. It's a surprisingly delicious mixture, so put aside your prejudices and try this modern version. The rose water, by the way, is not the modern triple distilled version familiar today, but a much milder version. If you're buying it, go to a chemist, and make sure you have the culinary kind.

INGREDIENTS

6 ozs short crust pastry

1 lb fresh spinach leaves, washed

8 ozs double cream

2 egg yolks

¼ lb currants

¼ lb caster sugar

½ teaspoon each ground cinnamon and rose water

METHOD

Plunge the spinach into a large saucepan of boiling salted water for 3 minutes. Drain it thoroughly and chop with the back of a knife in a colander to release all the liquid. Stir the 2 egg yolks into the cream, mix in the currants and the sugar, stirring until thoroughly blended. Add the spinach and stir again. Season with the cinnamon and rose water. Roll out the pastry and line an 8 inch diameter, 1 inch deep, tart tin. Pour the spinach mixture in and bake in a preheated oven, Gas Mark 5, 190°C, 375°F, for 35 to 40 minutes until the centre is well risen and brown. Test with a skewer to see that the filling is cooked right the way through and serve warm or cold.

A SPINAGE TART
Boyle your spinage and put to it half a pint of creame a Little Rose watter half a pound of currants a Little Cinamon and half a pound of suger then fill your tart to bake.

Hot Cross Buns

UNKNOWN, 1818

Hot cross buns are a tradition in Britain going back at least as far as the Reformation. Here is a simple country recipe, using the original method which simply marked the buns with a cross cut on the top and not with a separate coloured paste or marzipan. Likewise the buns were spiced and not fruited. I have indicated where you could add fruit if you have a mind to do so.

INGREDIENTS
(TO MAKE 8 BUNS)

1 lb strong flour

3 ozs caster sugar

1/2 teaspoon each ground coriander, cinnamon and mace

3 ozs butter

3 tablespoons milk

7 fl ozs warm water

1/2 oz fresh yeast

1/2 teaspoon salt

4 ozs currants and sultanas (optional)

1 teaspoon sunflower oil

FOR GLAZE

2 tablespoons milk, or 1 teaspoon sugar dissolved in water

METHOD

Warm the flour for five minutes in the oven set to Gas Mark 6, 200°C, 400°F. Mix the yeast with a pinch of the sugar and the milk. After about five to ten minutes, when it is frothy, mix it into the flour and add the warm water and the salt. Knead to a dough until the mixture is thoroughly incorporated. Rub a bowl with the oil to prevent the dough from sticking. Place the dough in the bowl and cover with a tea towel. Leave for about an hour in a warm place. Knead the dough again, adding the caster sugar, the spices and the butter. If using the currants and sultanas, add them to the dough at this stage. After kneading the dough thoroughly, cut it into 8, and roll each section between your palms. Place on a baking tray with enough room around them to spread, and press down gently. Allow to rise for another 15 to 20 minutes covered with a tea towel, then brush with the sugar and water (or milk) to glaze. Mark a cross on the top with a sharp knife and bake for 20 to 25 minutes in the oven till risen and brown.

TO MAKE CROSS BUNS
Put 2 lbs and a half of fine flour into a wooden Bowl, and set it before the fire to warm, then add half a lb of sifted sugar, some Coriander seed, Cinnamon & mace powdered fine, melt 1/2 a lb of butter, in 1/2 a pint of milk, when it is as warm as it will bear the finger, mix with it 3 tablespoonsful of very thick yeast and a little salt, put it to the flour, mix it to a paste and make the buns as directed in the last receipt*. Put a cross on the Top not very deep. (*To make Common Buns cover it over and set it before the fire an hour to rise, then make it into Buns, put them on a tin set them before the fire, for a quarter of an hour, cover over with flannel, then brush them with very warm milk, and bake them of a nice brown in a moderate oven).

Bisketts the Maidstone Way

MARSHAM FAMILY, THE MOTE, 17TH-18TH CENTURY

The Marsham family, whose recipe this is originally lived in Cuxton near Rochester on the Medway, but moved in the 18th century to the Mote at Mote Park in Maidstone. The house had previously been the home of the Woodvilles, the family of Elizabeth, Edward IV's queen. It seems likely that the Marshams' move up the river to Maidstone was the basis for this recipe for biscuits cooked in the county town's style. In culinary terms they're notable for having no fat in the recipe, but have quite exotic spicing.

INGREDIENTS

12 ozs flour

4 ozs ground almonds

1 teaspoon rose water

1 lb caster sugar

8 egg yolks, 4 egg whites (size 4 or 5)

1 teaspoon ground caraway and coriander

1 teaspoon caraway and coriander seeds

METHOD

Sift the flour into a mixing bowl. Add the ground almonds, ground spices, rosewater and the caster sugar and mix thoroughly. Beat the egg yolks and add them, and lightly beat the egg whites till thickened but not stiff. Fold them in, and spoon the mixture, a tablespoon at a time, into shallow greased patty pans. Strew a couple of each of the spice seeds over the top and bake in a Gas Mark 5 oven, 190°C, 375°F, for 12 minutes until lightly browned but not overcooked. They can also be baked flat on baking sheets using a tablespoon of mixture per biscuit.

> *BISKETTS THE MAIDSTONE WAY*
> *Take 3 quarters of a pound of Fine Flower, a quarter of a pound of Jordan almonds, blanch them and beat them very fine with 4 sponefulls of Rose water, then take a pound of loafe sugar beaten very fine mix all these well together then take eight eggs leaving out halfe the whites beate them very well, Then straw a few Coriander and Carriway seeds, Then put them in the panns and sift a little fine sugar over them then bake them in a warme oven.*

Imperial Pop

WOODGATE FAMILY, CHIDDINGSTONE, 1765

An excellent recipe for ginger beer, inscribed in the pages of a diary of 1756. Why it was called Imperial Pop at that time is difficult to say. It would have been a more likely name at the end of the 19th century when the British Empire had gained real momentum rather than in the 18th century. It comes from the Woodgate family who were rectors of Chiddingstone, near Anne Boleyn's and Henry VIII's Hever Castle. The rectory is still there although the manor house at Chiddingstone was overlaid with mock Gothic delusions of grandeur more than half a century after this recipe was written.

INGREDIENTS

1 oz root ginger

1 oz cream of tartar

Rind and juice of a lemon

1 lb caster sugar

6 pints water

2 ozs fresh yeast added to a little water to form a cream

METHOD

Severely bruise the ginger without peeling it, using the back of a heavy frying pan or a steak hammer. Place it, with the cream of tartar, the juice and grated rind of the lemon and the sugar into a large earthenware or glass jug or bowl. Do not use metal for this purpose. Pour the boiling water over them and stir well. When it is cool enough to dip your finger in without screaming, add the yeast mixture and stir till smoothly blended. Allow to cool and strain into glass bottles, preferably with solid screw tops. Screw down tight. Leave it for at least a week before you drink it.

THE WOODGATE FAMILY

The Woodgate family lived in and around Chiddingstone from early times. In the 18th and 19th centuries they were predominantly clergymen, but clergymen with very grand connections, as they were related to families connected with Penshurst and Broomham Park. The rectory where they lived still exists and is an interesting 18th century building. The author of the recipes is unknown but in some ways they are the most extraordinary in the book, because they are written into a printed diary of 1765 containing all kinds of information, admonitions and instructions for profiting from and enjoying the seasons. A number of these are printed throughout this book in facsimile form.

CHIDDINGSTONE

The village of Chiddingstone is now owned entirely by the National Trust. It has a number of fine 16th, 17th and 18th century houses and an extraordinary 'castle', which was the old High Street house, remodelled in the 19th century in a manner that can only be described as 'over grand Gothic'. Together with the church, which has an enormous tower, it forms a fascinating glimpse of an English village largely untouched by the 20th century.

IMPERIAL POP

One ounce of bruised Ginger - one ounce of Cream of Tartar - the juice of a Lemon - one pound of loaf Sugar, put these into a Jug or large Vessel - then pour four quarts of boiling Water over them & stir them well together, & when Milk warm, add two table Spoonfulls of Yeast - When quite cold, strain it thro' Muslin, Bottle it, cork it well & tie down the corks - It will be fit to drink the next Day.

Mr Butlers
Goosbery Wine

TWISDEN FAMILY, BRADBOURNE PARK, 1675-1750

This is an attributed recipe from the Twisden family cookery book and seems to come from the early 18th century. Who Mr Butler was is not known, but gooseberry wines have for centuries been a great country favourite. This must have been a particularly fine example to be noted with the donor's name.

INGREDIENTS

3 lbs gooseberries

1 1/2 pints water

1 lb caster sugar

METHOD

In a large non-metallic bowl, crush the gooseberries with your hands or a potato masher. Add the water, which you have brought to the boil, and let it stand in a warm place for 12 hours. Put it in a jelly bag, and allow to drip through. Discard the pulp. Add the sugar to the juice, stir till it is dissolved and leave to stand in a covered earthenware jug or bowl for 5 days. Skim off any debris before bottling in glass bottles with a good cork or seal. Leave the wine for at least 3 months in a cool dark place before drinking.

MR BUTLERS RECEIPT FOR GOOSBERY WINE

Take 3 pound of goosberys squeeze th(e)m in yo(u)r hands th(e)n one quart of boyld water to th(e)m & let them stand 12 hours press it w(i)t(h) a weight or your hands through flannell bag put a pound of suger to it & let it stand 4 or 5 days coverd skim it & put it in a vessell

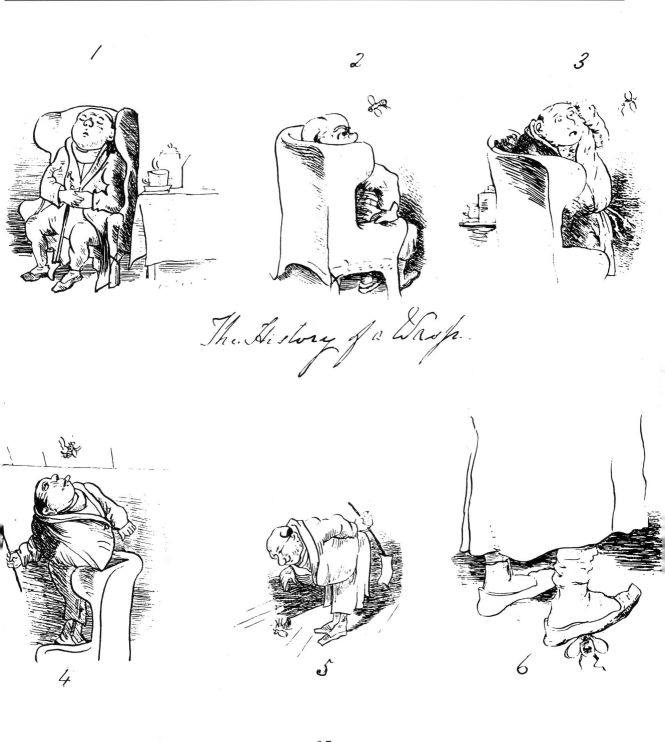

The History of a Wasp.

Obfervations on June, 1765.

Full Moon the 3d Day, at 5 in the Afternoon.
Laſt Quarter the 10th Day, at 10 in the Morning.
New Moon the 18th Day, at 11 in the Morning.
Firſt Quarter the 26th Day, at 9 in the Morning.

D	O R	O S	
1	3 57	8 3	Sow Broccoli the Beginning of
2	3 56	8 4	this Month for a ſecond Crop.
3	3 55	8 5	Tranſplant Sellery for blanching ;
4	3 55	8 5	tranſplant Cabbage and Savoy Plants
5	3 54	8 6	for Winter Uſe. Sow Kidney-
6	3 53	8 7	Beans and brown Dutch Cabbage-
7	3 53	8 7	Letuce for a late Crop.
8	3 52	8 8	
9	3 51	8 9	
10	3 51	8 9	Gather ſuch Herbs for drying as
11	3 50	8 10	are now in Flower, and let them
12	3 50	8 10	dry leiſurely in a ſhady Place, and
13	3 50	8 10	not in the Sun. Sow all Sorts of
14	3 49	8 11	ſmall Sallad Herbs every three or
15	3 49	8 11	four Days. Keep your Garden
16	3 48	8 12	free from all Sorts of Weeds, for
17	3 48	8 12	they ſpoil whatever Plants they are
18	3 48	8 12	near. Weed your Corn, and ſow
19	3 48	8 12	Rape, Cole-Seed, and Turnip-Seed
20	3 47	8 13	
21	3 47	8 13	
22	3 47	8 13	The Summer Quarter begins th.
23	3 48	8 12	21ſt of June, at 7 in the Morning.
24	3 48	8 12	
25	3 48	8 12	
26	3 48	8 12	Cooling Sallads, as Letuce, Sor-
27	3 48	8 12	rel, Purſlane, &c. will prevent too
28	3 49	8 11	great a Perſpiration, and throw off
29	3 49	8 11	feveriſh Diſorders.
30	3 50	8 10	

In the times before metalled roads and central heating, trains and telephones, Summer was a time of great freedom. Travel was possible, indeed often easy and pleasant, and living out of doors offered a relief from the closed houses and heavy clothes of Winter and early Spring. And not least, fresh foods were suddenly on the table again. A glance at the list of vegetables on the planting advice on this page will give you an idea of just what a cornucopia could suddenly appear. Salads were hugely popular and indeed one 17th century gardening and cookery book lists more then 24 different varieties of salad greens. We seem to have acquired an early taste for picnic food and eating out of doors as well in the Summer, even if the old story is true about sandwiches not having been invented until the 18th century Earl of the same name needed something to sustain him at the gaming tables.

By June the first fruits had begun to appear, particularly the great variety of berries with their short but intense season - a pleasure that is easy for us to forget with strawberries and cherries being flown in from all over the world whatever the time of year. So great was the delight in these brief periods of nature's bounty that they were often celebrated by festivals, and Kent in particular was famous for its cherry festivals where enormous amounts of the fruit would be consumed both raw and cooked into a variety of dishes but above all into pies and dumplings. Just one of the traditions that we have lost in exchange for continuous effortless supplies.

Obſervations on July, 1765.

Full Moon the 2d Day, at Midnight.
Laſt Quarter the 9th Day, at 10 at Night.
New Moon the 18th Day, at 1 in the Morning.
Firſt Quarter the 25th Day, at 4 in the Afternoon.

D	O R	O S	
1	3 51	8 10	
2	3 51	8 9	Sow Turnips and Onions to ſtand
3	3 51	8 9	the Winter ; as alſo Carrots, Cole-
4	3 52	8 8	worts and Cauliflowers. Keep your
5	3 53	8 7	Garden clean from Weeds, and do
6	3 53	8 7	not neglect to weed in this Month
7	3 53	8 7	your new-planted Quicks.
8	3 54	8 6	
9	3 55	8 5	
10	3 56	8 4	
11	3 57	8 3	
12	3 58	8 2	Gather ſuch Seeds as are ripe, as
13	3 59	8 1	alſo Flowers, and dry them in the
14	4 8	8 0	Shade, and then in the Sun.
15	4 1	7 59	
16	4 2	7 58	
17	4 3	7 57	
18	4 4	7 56	
19	4 5	7 55	
20	4 6	7 54	
21	4 8	7 52	
22	4 9	7 51	
23	4 10	7 50	
24	4 12	7 48	Forbear ſuperfluous Drinking.
25	4 13	7 47	Uſe cold Herbs. Shun boil'd, ſalt
26	4 15	7 45	and ſtrong Meats, and abſtain from
27	4 16	7 44	Phyſick.
28	4 18	7 42	
29	4 19	7 41	
30	4 21	7 39	
31	4 22	7 38	

Obſervations on Auguſt, 1765.

Full Moon the 1ſt Day, at 7 in the Morning.
Laſt Quarter the 8th Day, at 1 in the Afternoon.
New Moon the 16th Day, at 4 in the Afternoon.
Firſt Quarter the 23d Day, at 11 at Night.
Full Moon the 30th Day, at 4 in the Afternoon.

D	O R	O S	
1	4 24	7 36	
2	4 25	7 35	
3	4 27	7 33	Sow Cauliflowers, Spinage, O-
4	4 28	7 32	nions, Cabbages, Coleworts, Le-
5	4 30	7 30	tuce, Creſſes, Chervil, and Corn-
6	4 32	7 28	Sallad, for Winter Uſe. Tranſ-
7	4 33	7 27	plant Broccoli into the Ground,
8	4 35	7 25	where it is to remain for flowering.
10	4 38	7 22	Plant Slips of Savory, Thyme, Sage,
11	4 41	7 19	Hyſſop, Roſemary, Lavender, Ma-
12	4 43	7 17	ſtick, and other aromatick Plants.
14	4 45	7 15	Continue to ſow Rape, Radiſh,
15	4 47	7 13	Muſtard, Creſſes, and Turnip-Seed,
16	4 49	7 11	every Week ; they will now ſoon
17	4 50	7 10	grow large enough for Uſe.
18	4 52	7 8	
19	4 54	7 6	
20	4 56	7 4	This Month uſe moderate Diet,
21	4 58	7 2	forbear to ſleep ſoon after Meat ;
22	4 57	7 3	for that brings Opilations, Head-
23	5 1	6 59	achs, Agues, and Cathars, and o-
24	5 3	6 57	ther Diſtempers of the ſame Kind.
25	5 5	6 55	Take great Care of ſudden Cold
26	5 7	6 53	after Heat.
27	5 9	6 51	
28	5 10	6 50	
29	5 12	6 48	
30	5 14	6 46	
31	5 16	6 44	

summer

Green Pease Soop

WHATMAN FAMILY, BOXLEY, 1820

At first this seemed to be a Lenten soup, meant for the forty days before Easter when meat was forbidden. But the use of fresh peas, which would not have been available under normal conditions until at least June, makes this undoubtedly a Summer dish rather than one from penitent Lent. There is another peculiarity in that the dish seems to be, both in its cooking style and in the writing, much older than the 1820 date that the book of recipes from the Whatman family from Boxley in Maidstone would suggest. The family had connections with Knole and the Sackvilles but, perhaps more significant, Boxley was the site of the great Cistercian Abbey founded by William de Ypres, Earl of Kent, in the 12th century. It was razed to the ground at the dissolution of the monasteries in 1538 but the style of the dish suggests possible monastic origins. Throuhout the year as well as in Lent, Cistercian and Benedictine monks used peas as a staple, fresh and dried. Whatever its origins, it is a very delicate and intensely green soup, well worth trying in this modern form.

INGREDIENTS

2 lbs green peas, shelled

1/2 lb onions, peeled and chopped

1/2 teaspoon each ginger, cloves, mace and black pepper
2 sprigs of mint, chopped

8 spinach leaves, washed and sliced into quarter inch ribbons

8 lettuce leaves, washed and sliced into quarter inch ribbons

1 dessertspoon each of butter and plain flour

1 pint water

Salt and pepper

Croutons, made from 2 slices of white bread, fried light brown in a little oil

METHOD

Put aside about a third of the peas, separating the small, delicate and sweet peas. Place the rest in a saucepan with the onion, spices and half the mint. Add 1 pint of water, together with the spinach and lettuce leaves and simmer till the peas are soft. Purée the mixture in a liquidiser until it is as smooth as possible. Blanch the young peas for three minutes and add them to the mixture, with the rest of the mint. Bring it to the boil, and simmer for 5 minutes. Mash the butter and flour together, and stir that into the soup over a very slow simmer.

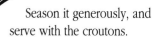

Season it generously, and serve with the croutons.

GREEN PEASE SOOP WITHOUT MEAT

In shelling your pease seperate the young from the old, then take the Old ones and set them to boil with a little water, 2 large Onyons, a blade or two of Mace, a little bit of Ginger and two or three Cloves, & whole pepper, and a Sprig of Mint, the Young Pease must be boil'd by themselves, & you must have some Spinage, Lettuce, and mint and a little Charville boil'd to be tender, strain the liquor & pulp from the Old pease, and when it is just ready to boil, put in the young pease, & herbs, when it boils up have ready some butter mix'd with flour to thicken it, you must not let it boil long after the butter is put in, or it will seperate - Salt it to your taste, & put in a french role, or toast as you like -

To CLEAN KID GLOVES.—First; see that your hands are clean, then put on your gloves and wash them, as though you were washing your hands, in a basin of turpentine, until quite clean; then hang them up in a warm place, or where there is a good current of air, which will carry off all smell of the turpentine. This method was brought from Paris, and thousands of pounds have been made by it.

CURE FOR THE TOOTHACHE.—Take a piece of sheet zinc, about the size of a sixpence, and a piece of silver, say a shilling; place them together, and hold the defective tooth between or contiguous to them; in a few minutes the pain will be gone, as if by magic. The zinc and silver, acting as a galvanic battery, will produce on the nerves of the tooth sufficient electricity to establish a current, and, consequently, to relieve the pain.

To CLEAN BLACK SATIN.—In a quart of water boil three pounds of potatoes to a pulp. Strain the water through a sieve, and brush the satain with it, upon a board or table. The material is not to be wrung, but folded down in cloths for three hours, and then ironed on the wrong side.

Potted Shrimps

HUSSEY FAMILY, SCOTNEY CASTLE, EARLY 19TH CENTURY

The Medway, and indeed the whole of the North Kent coast , used to be famous for its pink and brown shrimps. In the early 19th century, when this recipe was collected by the Husseys at Scotney Castle, crabs, oysters, winkles and shrimps were so plentiful that people used to make special journeys to sample the Thames and Medway estuary sea food. It can still be found in one or two specialised shops if you know where to look, in Whitstable and Sittingbourne.

This recipe makes a marvellous starter, potted in individual ramekins, or a splendid centre piece for high tea if you choose to make one large dish of it. Serve with lots of wholemeal toast - you won't need much butter.

INGREDIENTS

1 lb fresh shrimps (not prawns, they should be approx the length of the top joint of your little finger)

1/2 teaspoon powdered mace

1/4 teaspoon white pepper
1 teaspoon salt

1/2 lb butter

METHOD

Mix the spices, salt and shrimps together and let them stand for 2 hours in a glass or china bowl. Add 1 oz of the butter and put the bowl into a saucepan with water a couple of inches up the side. Cover and steam for 40 minutes. Melt the butter in a pan. Remove the heads from the shrimps and discard. Their tails are sufficiently softened by the cooking process not to be a problem. Place the shrimps in individual ramekins, or a large communal dish, and pour the butter carefully over them, leaving the white residue in the bottom of the saucepan. Make sure the shrimps are covered, and allow to cool for an hour before chilling in the fridge for 2 hours at least. They will keep for 3 to 4 days.

TO POTT SHRIMPS

To a p[oun]d of Shrimps put one Dram of Mase and h[al]f a Dram of Black Pepper well beat put a little Salt and mix it well together. Let them stand two Hours then put them in a Pitsher with one onz of Butter over the Pitsher and put it into a Kettle of Water and Stew four hours then Heat the Shrimps well put in h[al]f a p[oun]d of clarified Butter pot them whole. Cover them with Butter.

Potted Salmon

THE WOLFE FAMILY
General Sir James Wolfe is the famous member of his family. He died at the extraordinarily young age of 30, at the moment when a British army under his command had secured victory on the Heights of Abraham, making Canada a British and not a French colony. His early life was spent in Westerham where he was born in the Rector's house, and where he grew up, partly in his own home and partly in the home of his friends, the young Wardes who lived at Squerryes Court. His mother was a friend of the Warde family and it is fitting that her cookery book is still preserved at the house where her son received his commission. Her recipes show her particular interest in the cooking of fish.

Take the middle piece of any Salmon. Season it with salt pepper cloves mace a few bay leaves. Put it in a pot with as much melted butter as will cover it. Set it in the oven with small bread. When it is baked take it out o' th' pot put it in the pot you keep it in pour the butter of it was baked in. Clarifie it & pour it on the Salmon. If you find it not high enough seasoned put more seasoning in ye pot you keep it in. The same way you may pot eels or trouts only of those fish you must take out the bones.

SQUERRYES COURT
Squerryes Court dates from the 1680s and since 1731 it has been the home of the Warde family, who still cherish and enjoy it. It's open to the public and has a remarkable collection of pictures, starting with a picture of Philip II of Spain. The Darent rises in the gardens of Squerryes and since its visitors also have the chance to visit Quebec House just up the road, where Wolfe's family lived, this makes Westerham an ideal town for a dip into history.

Potted Salmon

MRS WOLFE, WESTERHAM, 18TH CENTURY

This recipe almost certainly has the distinction of having been eaten by one of Britain's great national heroes, General Wolfe, hero of the victory on the Heights of Abraham at Quebec which finally gave Britain control of Canada. Wolfe was born in Westerham and his mother's cookery book is still to be seen in the elegant house of one of her neighbours at Squerryes Court. This recipe was written at the beginning of the eighteenth century when salmon was still commonplace in the clean rivers of southern England. Modern fish farming techniques have made them almost as widely available again today as they were then. But potting fish, or indeed meats, was not at that time as it so often is today a way of using up leftovers; it was a way of cooking and preserving food before the time of refrigeration. This salmon makes a marvellous first course with hot toast, or can also be an excellent main course eaten with salad and hot potatoes. Scrape most of the butter off if you are eating it in this second way, because the butter adds flavour but is not meant to be a substantial part of the dish.

INGREDIENTS

1¹/2 - 2 lb cut of salmon, across the whole fish

1¹/2 teaspoons salt

1 teaspoon white pepper

¹/2 teaspoon each cloves and mace

4 bay leaves

1¹/2 lbs butter or cooking butter

METHOD

Wash and trim the salmon thoroughly and, if you or your fishmonger have the skill, skin it without cutting it up any further. Season it generously with the salt and spices. Place two bayleaves in the cavity, and one at the bottom of a baking dish or casserole into which the salmon will only just fit. Place the other bayleaf on top. Melt the butter and pour over the salmon, making sure that it is covered. Cover the pot or casserole and put it in a preheated Gas Mark 4, 180°C, 350°F, oven. Bake for 45 - 50 minutes until the fish is thoroughly cooked. Remove carefully from the dish. You can at this time, if you like, bone it and skin it if you haven't done so before. Be careful not to break the flesh up. Place it in a serving dish with sides high enough to allow you to pour the butter it has cooked in over it. If you wish to keep it for some time, the butter should once again cover the fish. You may need to add some more butter as you do this. Only pour in the clear oil, leaving the white residues, herbs and seasonings aside. Allow to cool for an hour and chill in the fridge. When it is cold you may cover it with clingfilm or foil. It will keep, chilled and lightly covered, for up to 2 weeks before using. (The original recipe points out that you may pot other river fish - eels or trout - like this, but you should in that case use only the fillets.)

Salma Gundy

HUSSEY FAMILY, SCOTNEY CASTLE, EARLY 19TH CENTURY

Salmagundy, or to give it its proper name, Salamangundi, was given its original title by Rabelais, that literary celebrator of excess. In fact, although this recipe from the Hussey family is quite moderate, Salmagundy could be a most elaborate hors d'oeuvre. That is how it was traditionally eaten. Normally, it would have contained more fresh ingredients, in contrast to the pickled herrings and boiled eggs of the Hussey version. So my suggestion takes its inspiration from the original recipe, but is more adjusted to our lighter tastes and palates, and our pleasure in freshness.

Conventionally salmagundy was built up into a kind of sugar cone confection based on a big basin in the middle of the table. Jane Grigson's view, following Hannah Glasse, was that the individual items are nicest in separate bowls, but I must say that I prefer the impact of the built up plate. Salmagundy is delicious eaten with a variety of breads - wholemeal and french provide a nice contrast. Each person helps themselves to a segment of the Salmagundy as though taking a section from a cake.

> Take the white part of a roasted Chicken the yolks of four boiled Eggs and the whites of the same & pickled Herrings and a handful of Parsley chop them seperately exceeding small take the same quantity of lean boiled Ham scraped fine turn a China Bason upsidedown in the midle of a Dish make a qu⁫. of a pound of Butter in to the shape of a Pine Apple and set it on the top of the Bason lay round the Bason a ring of Parsley then a ring of yolks of Eggs then of the Whites then Ham then Chicken then Herring till you have covered your Bason and used all your ingredients garnish it with Capers and Oysters

INGREDIENTS

2 chicken breasts, cooked and skinned

4 hard boiled eggs, finely chopped

2 rollmops, finely chopped

1 cucumber

2 eating apples, cored but not peeled

2 large pickled gherkins, chopped

1 bunch of watercress, washed

4 sticks of celery, scrubbed

2 tablespoons white wine vinegar

8 tablespoons oil, olive or other salad oil

2 tablespoons lemon juice

1 teaspoon salt

1 teaspoon sugar, 4 table-spoons parsley, chopped

2 tablespoons capers, roughly chopped

METHOD

Begin by making two dressings, one of them lemon and the other vinegar. Place half the oil, half the salt, all of the sugar and the lemon juice in one pot and shake thoroughly. Place the remaining oil and salt in a second pot with the vinegar, and shake thoroughly.

Cut the chicken breasts into half inch cubes. Cut the celery stalks once lengthwise, and then across into quarter inch pieces. Cut the cucumber once lengthwise, scoop out and discard the seeds, and then slice the halves crosswise into quarter inch slices. Cut the apples into rings approximately a quarter inch thick. On a large oval dish place a soup plate or small basin (upside down) in the middle. Pile the finely chopped herring onto the top of it, and surround with a sprinkling of parsley. Pile the chicken cubes around the base of the basin, piling them up as close to it as possible. Place the hardboiled eggs in a ring around the chicken and garnish with the gherkins. Dip the apple rings in the lemon dressing and arrange around the basin in an atttractive pattern between the hard boiled eggs and the chopped herring. Mix the celery with the remaining lemon dressing. Mix the cucumber with the vinegar dressing, and add the capers. Arrange the celery, and the cucumber and capers, around the dish in alternate rings on top of the other ingredients. Sprinkle the whole with the watercress leaves, filling in any gaps, and making as attractive a pattern as you can.

TO MAKE SALMA GUNDY
Take the white part of a roasted Chicken the yolks of four boiled Eggs and the whites of the same 2 pickled Herrings and a handful of Parsley chop them seperately exceeding small take the same quantity of lean boiled Ham scrape'd fine turn a China Bason upside down in the middle of a Dish make a qu[arte]r of a pound of Butter into the shape of a Pine Apple and set it on the top of the Bason lay round the Bason a ring of Parsley then a ring of yolks of Eggs then of whites then Ham then Chicken then Herring till you have covered your Bason and used all your ingredients garnish it with Capers and Oysters.

Caveach

HUSSEY FAMILY, SCOTNEY CASTLE, 19TH CENTURY

Caveach is a dish that has a large number of relatives. It's a way of pickling fish that was widely used throughout Europe from Renaissance times onwards. The style still exists, most vividly, on the other side of the Atlantic in the Jamaican Escovitch fish, and the Mexican and Ecuadorian Seviche. At its best it's a very delicate dish where fish is lightly pickled in spiced vinegar, and served either as a starter or as part of a buffet dinner. This 19th century recipe probably marks the end in Britain of a long tradition of fish prepared like this; it should be revived.

INGREDIENTS

2 large mackerel, filleted

1 teaspoon salt

1 teaspoon white pepper

1/2 teaspoon powdered mace

2 tablespoons sunflower oil

1/2 pint cider vinegar

2 bay leaves

1 onion peeled and finely sliced

1 carrot peeled and finely sliced

METHOD

Trim the mackerel fillets and cut each one in half across. Heat the oil in a big frying pan, and fry the fillets, skin side down to start with, for 2 to 3 minutes on each side. Place the fillets in a shallow dish, season with the pepper, salt and mace, and set them aside to cool. Place the carrot and onion in the vinegar with the bay leaves, and bring to the boil. Allow the vinegar to cool below blood heat, and pour over the mackerel. Add more vinegar until the mackerel are completely submerged. Pour a drop or two of oil on the top to act as a seal, cover with clingfilm and refrigerate for 3 days. They will be fine to eat for up to another 8 to 10 days if kept covered in the fridge.

SEA TACKLE.

RODS, REELS, LINES, MOUNTED LINES for PIER, COAST, and DEEP

THE BERESFORD SEA FISHING OUTFIT.

For Rod or Hand Work.

Contents—

2 sea rods.
2 „ reels.
2 Bate's lines.
Conger line fitted.
Mackerel „ „
General „ „
4 paternosters.
4 traces.
Tackle box.
2 Deal leads.
2 Mahted leads.
Knife and gag.
6 mackerel spinners.
4 sand eels.
1 wagtail.
1 silver sand eel.
100 eyed hooks, assorted.
3 doz. swivels.
3 „ mounted hooks.
1 „ sea flies.
Fitted gaff.
Disgorger.
Cutting board.

£5 10 0

TO MAKE CAVEACH

Take of the largest Mackerel when they are full rood any number you please cut each into about 3 or 4 pieces season each piece well with pepper and Salt and a little Mace then fry them in oil till quite enough set them by till cold then put them into a pan of cold Vinegar with a handfull of bay leaves in it - there must be Vinegar enough to cover it with and pour some Oil on the Top and when they have stood 4 or 5 days they will be fit to eat.

Curry

GAMBIER FAMILY, LANGLEY, 1808

The Gambier family lived in Langley, close to Leeds Castle. They were a family of parsons who married into the Venn family, themselves well known Evangelical Divines in the 19th century, but their connections were worldwide, including Admirals and members of the House of Lords. It's not known from which connection this very sophisticated Indian curry recipe came, but it's clearly a recipe that had just come from India as it has none of the Anglo-Indian fripperies. It's delicious eaten with a big bowl of boiled rice and some cucumber and tomato salad in yoghurt. A little mango chutney is ok too, although it certainly wouldn't have been contemporary with this turn of the 19th century recipe.

INGREDIENTS

1 large chicken, jointed and skinned

2 ozs butter

2 ozs oil

1 lb onions, peeled and sliced

1 teaspoon ground turmeric

1 dessertspoon each ground ginger and black pepper

1/2 teaspoon each ground coriander and chilli powder

1 pint chicken or beef stock

Juice of 1 lemon

3 tablespoons cream or Greek yoghurt

Pinch of sugar - optional

METHOD

Melt the butter in the oil and fry the onions in them till pale gold. Add the chicken and fry till lightly brown, then add the spices and fry again for 2 to 3 minutes. Add the stock (or water) and simmer gently for 20 to 25 minutes. Add the lemon juice and check for seasoning. A small pinch of sugar may help the balance. Add the cream or yoghurt and stir it in just before serving.

CURRY

Take a large Chicken or Fowl, cut it up as for a Fricassee; skin the pieces, put 1/2lb of fresh Butter into a frying pan and fry 3 or 4 Onions quite tender, but dont let them be brown, drain them: then fry the Chicken in the same butter of a fine light brown then put the Chicken & Onions into a stew pan with 1/2 oz of Turmeric, 1/2 a Table spoonful of black Pepper, the same quantity of Ginger, and a few Coriander Seeds (all of which must be beaten and Sifted) & 1/2 a Tea Spoonfull of Cayenne pepper: Stew it all well together in a pint of good Beef Gravy, let it stew 1/2 hour: then add the juice of a large lemon. Keep stirring it that it may not stick to the pan. Just as you are going to dish it up, put in about 3 Table Spoonfuls of good Cream. It must not be put on the fire after the Cream is added as it would curdle.

Pale Frigasy

WOODGATE FAMILY, CHIDDINGSTONE, 1765

Obviously from its name this was a dish derived from France although in that country it would probably be known as a Blanquette. The Woodgate family from Chiddingstone (now a complete village preserved by the National Trust) appear to have regarded it as a catch-all recipe for any meat that happened to come to hand, but it's undoubtedly nicest made with lamb. It is interesting to see that this is identified separately from mutton in this mid-18th century recipe. It is very nice with early new potatoes and carrots or broad beans.

INGREDIENTS

2 lb lamb fillet or boned shoulder, cut into walnut sized pieces

Bouquet garni of bay leaf, sprig of thyme, sprig of parsley, celery leaf

1 spanish onion cut in half

3 eggs

1/2 teaspoon ground nutmeg

1 tablespoon chopped parsley

1 tablespoon butter

4 tablespoons double cream

1 teaspoon salt

METHOD

Place the lamb in a thick saucepan. Barely cover with water, adding a teaspoon of salt, the bouquet garni, and the onion. Bring to the boil, skim off any foam, turn it down to a very low simmer and cover. Cook for 25 minutes. Remove the meat to a warm dish. Beat the eggs together with the cream, add a ladleful of the stock and mix thoroughly. Put back in the pan, and bring gently towards the boil. Before it bubbles, add the butter, the nutmeg and the chopped parsley and stir together until thick. Don't let it boil ! When it has thickened, extract the bouquet garni and onion, and pour the sauce over the lamb to serve.

A PALE FRIGASY

Take Lamb Chicken or Rabbets cut in peices & wash it well from the blood th[e]n put it into a broad pan with as much fair Water as will Cover it, put in Salt a bunch of sweet herbs some pepper one onion two anchovies. Stew it till enough, then mix in a bason 6 yolks of Eggs a[n]d a glass of White Wine a Nutmeg grated a little choped parsley a bit of fresh butter and 4 or 5 spoonfuls of Cream beat all these together, & put it into y[ou]r pan shake it together till thick enough

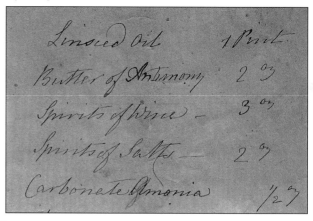

Linseed Oil — 1 Pint

Butter of Antimony — 2 oz

Spirits of Wine — 3 oz

Spirits of Salts — 2 oz

Carbonate Amonia — 1/2 oz

White Fricassee

WHATMAN FAMILY, BOXLEY, 1820

Although sharing the same name with the previous recipe, this really is a fricassee with the meat being fried first and sauced after. It's a later recipe, coming from around 1820, collected by the Whatman family who lived near Maidstone. If you make the fricassee with chicken breasts it becomes quite a grand dinner party dish. The recommendation to soak the meat to draw out the blood by the way is not necessary with modern chickens. It's best not made with the maize-fed golden chickens, so as to preserve the whiteness of the appearance. It is delicious with pasta, and eaten with something vividly green like spinach or broccoli.

INGREDIENTS

4 chicken breasts, skinned

4 tablespoons flour

1 tablespoon butter

1 tablespoon olive oil

1 blade of mace

1 teaspoon peppercorns

Bouquet garni of sprig of thyme, celery leaf, sprig of parsley, 2 bay leaves

1 pint chicken stock (can be made from a cube)

1 teaspoon celery salt

5 ozs double cream, 2 egg yolks, beaten, & 1 level dessertspoon cornflour mixed with a little water, whisked together

1/4 lb button mushrooms, sliced

METHOD

Melt the butter in the oil. Dredge the chicken breasts with the flour and fry gently until they are firm but not at all brown - covering the pan helps to achieve this. Add the mace, peppercorns, celery salt, bouquet garni and the chicken stock and simmer very gently for 20 minutes. Remove the breasts and place in a dish to keep warm. Remove the bouquet garni, blade of mace, and peppercorns, and measure off half a pint of the stock into a pan. Add the double cream, the egg yolks and cornflour. Bring it gently to the boil, stirring all the time until it is thickened. Place the button mushrooms in the remaining liquid stock, and bring to the boil quickly for one minute. Add the mushrooms to the sauce, and pour over the chicken breasts.

A WHITE FRICASSEE
When your Chickens are cut as you like them lay them in warm water to draw out the blood, & when they are perfectly drawn dry them in a Cloth - put a piece of butter the size of a Wallnut with a little flower in a stew pan to melt but it must not be the least brown then put in the Chicken with a blade of mace, a little whole pepper, & a small bundle of sweet-herbs cover them with white broth, or if you have not any very nice Warm Water - let them stew till they are tender then put in a quarter of a pint of cream the Yolks of 2 eggs & a few mushrooms, & keep it stirring all one way till 'tis of a proper thickness -

Beefsteaks

To Fry Beefe Steaks

TWISDEN FAMILY, BRADBOURNE PARK, LATE 17TH CENTURY

This recipe, on close inspection, turns out to be three separate recipes, each of them worthy of attention in its own right. It comes from the Twisden family who lived at Bradbourne Park in East Malling. The recipes were collected by a lady who described herself as " a Discrete Oulde and Maiden Gentlewoman" but she certainly knew a thing or two about cooking. The first two recipes, although they don't say it, are obviously designed to cope with tender and then tougher steaks by alternative methods. It's an early bit of writing and seems to have strong English roots, appropriately enough for a beef dish using ale rather than wine as the cooking medium. Here are all three modern recipes derived from the original.

INGREDIENTS

4 x 6 - 8 oz rump steaks

1 onion, peeled and finely chopped

1 teaspoon thyme and parsley, chopped

1/4 teaspoon grated nutmeg

1 dessertspoon each butter and flour, mashed together

1 teacup light ale or lager

Salt and pepper

METHOD

Heat a large, thick non stick pan until seriously hot. If the steak will benefit from it, pound them gently with a rolling pin. Trim the fat and place steaks in the hot pan, searing them for 30 to 60 seconds on each side. Allow them to loosen with their own juices before trying to turn them. Season generously. Add the onion and the herbs. Pour over the lager or ale and simmer for 2 to 3 minutes depending on how rare the steaks want to be. Remove the steaks and add the butter and flour. Stir until the sauce thickens and serve it with the steaks.

TO FRY BEEFE STEAKS

Take rump stakes beat th[e]m well with a rowler, fry th[e]m in half a pint of Ale, or moore sprinkle th[e]m with salt & oynion or onion cut small, when fryed enough ad savory, time, parsley & shalot, w[i]th a little onion & nutmeg chopt very small w[hi]ch role up in a piece of butter w[i]th flower, shade [sic] it up very thick & then serve it in. or thus half boyle yo[u]r stakes then put th[e]m into a stew pan cover th[e]m w[i]th gravey season th[e]m very well role up in the hearbs, shalot, onion & nutmeg in butter w[i]th flower & thicken it w[i]th y[ou]r yolk of an egg & so serve it in. y[o]u may draw gravey from an ox kidney cut in 2 or 3 pieces & seasoned high with salt & peper an onion, some sweet hearbs & butter putting water or wine to it enough to Cover it, & so gentley stewing it.

Stewed Steak

TWISDEN FAMILY, BRADBOURNE PARK, 1675-1750

INGREDIENTS

1¹/₂ lbs stewing steak, cut into inch thick slices

1 teaspoon thyme and parsley, chopped

1 cup light ale or lager

1 cup strong beef stock (not Oxo)

¹/₄ teaspoon grated nutmeg

1 dessertspoon each butter and flour, mashed together

1 tablespoon cooking oil

METHOD

Heat the oil in a sautée or frying pan and quickly brown the beef steaks in it. Add the lager or beer and simmer for 5 minutes. Add the stock, herbs and onion and simmer for about 25 minutes or until the meat is tender. Remove the steaks to a serving dish, add the nutmeg to the liquids, and stir in the butter and flour over a low heat until the sauce is thickened.

Ox Kidney Sautée

TWISDEN FAMILY, BRADBOURNE PARK, 1675-1750

INGREDIENTS

1¹/₂ lbs Ox kidney

1 teaspoon salt

I teaspoon ground black pepper

1 large onion, roughly chopped

1 dessertspoon each fresh marjoram and thyme, chopped

2 tablespoons butter

1 tablespoon cornflour, mixed with a little water

METHOD

Remove any fat and skin from the kidney and cut it into pieces the size of a walnut. Season generously with the salt and pepper and fry it in the butter till lightly browned. Add the onion and the herbs and just enough water to cover. Simmer gently for 45 minutes. Stir the cornflour into the juices bringing the sauce to a light boil until it is thickened. Check for further seasoning.

Stewed Rump Steaks

More than a hundred and fifty years later an almost identical recipe turns up in the Roper manuscripts collected by a Mrs D Tyler about 1840. I don't give a modern version as it's almost identical to the stewed steak recipe from the 17th century, the refinement being the use of ½ lb button onions as a garnish and cooking the meat in claret or port wine instead of ale.

Croquet at Chevening in 1862.

G. Scharf

STEWED RUMP STEAKS

The Steaks must be a little thicker than for broiling let them be all of the same thickness, or some will be done too much and others too little - Put an oz of butter into a Stewpan, with two Onions; when the Butter is melted put in the Rump Steaks, let them stand over a slow fire for five minutes then turn them, and let the other side of them fry five minutes longer Have ready boiled a point of Button Onions they will take from half an hour to an hour put the liquor they were boiled in to the Steaks if there is not enough of it to cover them, add broth or boiling water, to make up enough for that purpose, with a dozen corns of Black Pepper and a little salt and let them simmer very gently for about an hour and a half and then strain off as much of the liquor as you think will make the same. Put 2oz butter into a Stewpan, when it is melted, stir in as much flour as will make it into a stiff paste; some add thereto a tablespoonful of Claret or Port Wine, the same of Mushroom Catsup half a teaspoonful of Salt, and a quarter of a tea spoonful of ground black pepper: add the liquor by degrees, let it boil up for fifteen minutes; skim it, and strain it serve up the steaks with the Onions round the dish and pour the gravy over

Sauce Robart

UNKNOWN, 1818

If you prefer just to grill your steaks, and throughout English history we've liked our beef cooked pretty simply, here's an interesting sauce designed to go with a grilled steak. The name's particularly interesting as it's clearly an early version, both in spelling and in method, of a sauce made famous by Escofier nearly a century later under the name of Sauce Robert: was he perhaps, in his time in England, a researcher amongst ancient cookery books?

INGREDIENTS

1 tablespoon butter

4 ozs onion, peeled and very finely chopped

1 dessertspoon plain flour

8 tablespoons beef stock

1 teaspoon made mustard

1 tablespoon cider vinegar

Juice of half a lemon

METHOD

Place the butter in a non-stick saucepan and heat it until pale gold - do not let it burn! Add the onion and turn the heat down immediately. Add the flour and stir it thoroughly, then add the beef stock and blend with a whisk. Season generously and simmer it for 10 minutes to cook the flour. Allow to cool and then add the mustard, vinegar and lemon juice. Bring it up to the boil and use it to sauce the steaks. (If made in double or treble quantities it keeps well in a sealed jar in the fridge.)

SAUCE ROBART, FOR RUMPS OR STEAKS

Put a peice of butter, the size of an egg, into a saucepan, set it over the fire, and when browning, throw in a hanful of sliced onions cut small, fry them brown but do not let them burn, add half a spoonful of flour, shake the onions in it, and give it another fry, then put 4 spoonsful of gravy, and some pepper and salt, and boil it gently ten minutes, when cold, skim off the fat, add a teaspoonful of made mustard, a spoonful of vinegar and the juice of half a lemon, boil it all, and pour it round the steaks. They should be of a fine yellow brown and garnished with fried parsley and Lemon.

To Stew Cucumbers

HUSSEY FAMILY, SCOTNEY CASTLE, EARLY 19TH CENTURY

We tend to think of cucumbers as essentially a salad vegetable, but in many parts of the world, and in Britain for many centuries before this one, they were eaten cooked as often as raw. This was not least because the varieties available tended not to be the hothouse burpless kind we are familiar with now. Cooking, it was believed, had a beneficial effect on their windiness. This dish is a particularly nice addition to grilled chicken or fish.

INGREDIENTS

2 large cucumbers

2 tablespoons butter

1 blade of mace

6 fl ozs chicken stock

1 dessertspoon each butter and plain flour, mashed together

Salt and pepper

METHOD

Cut the cucumbers in half lengthwise, scoop out the seeds and slice across into half inch pieces. Heat the butter in a large frying pan until it foams and add the cucumber slices and fry for 2 to 2½ minutes. Remove them with a slotted spoon to warm dish. Place the chicken stock and mace into the pan and bring it to the boil. Over a low heat stir the butter and flour into the sauce. Add the cucumber, check for seasoning, simmer 1 minute and serve immediately while they are still somewhat crisp.

TO STEW CUCUMBERS

Pare them and slice them pretty thick fry them in fresh Butter drain them on a sive put them in a Stew Pan with a large Glass of red Wine the same quantity of Gravy a blade of Mace thicken it with flour and Butter when it boils put in your Cucumbers keep shaking them 5 Minutes will do them.

Tomata Catchup

GAMBIER FAMILY, LANGLEY, 1843

Ketchup, or catsup, are all variations on the spelling for what was in the 17th and 18th centuries a strong dark sauce, rather like Worcestershire sauce, made from walnuts and/or mushrooms. By 1843, when this recipe was recorded, it had come to mean a tomato based sauce unless mushrooms were specified. Tomatoes had only really just gained widespread acceptance and distribution, having been held for many years after their arrival from the New World, as having dangerous and aphrodisiac properties. Nowadays we regard tomato sauce as something that's always bought in the shop but this delicious and quite highly spiced version is sophisticated enough to be used as something other than simply a dipping sauce for chips. The original was made on rather a grand scale with 2 gallons of tomatoes, something like 16 lbs, as the basis. This modern version will make about 3 pints of ketchup to be stored in glass jars or screw top bottles. The recommendation for shaking before using is still good centuries later.

INGREDIENTS

4 lbs ripe tomatoes

1½ ozs salt

1 teaspooon each ground cloves, black pepper and ginger

½ pint cider vinegar

2 cloves of garlic, crushed

METHOD

Cut the tomatoes in half and place them in a china or glass bowl and put the salt over them. Let them stand overnight out of the fridge. Place them in a saucepan and cook gently for an hour until completely soft. Process them or put them through a mouli legumes, add the spices and the garlic. Add the vinegar and stir the mixture thoroughly. Let it simmer for another 45 minutes to 1 hour and bottle while warm in sterilised glass jars.

TOMATA CATCHUP

Add a handful of Salt to a peck of Tomatoes let them stand all night: put them into a stewpan & let them boil gently for 2 hours, then rub them thro' a hair sieve. To a gallon of the Liquor add of Cloves, Black Pepper & Ginger one oz: A pint of Vinegar & salt to your taste After this is done let it boil for 2 hours more, & when boiled throw in a few garlics or eschalots - When cold put it into small bottles Shake it well before each time of using.

English Fresh Cheese

MARSHAM FAMILY, WHORNES PLACE, 17TH-18TH CENTURY

This summer cheese recipe, to be made with the rich summer milk, is a tradition we've lost in Britain but continues to this day unabated in France where coeurs à la crême are still made and eaten in almost exactly the same way. The only difference being that the French version, and indeed some other early English versions, contemporary with this Marsham family recipe from the early 17th century, contain beaten egg whites as well. This is a delicate dish which, in modern France, and perhaps in Cromwell's or Charles II's England, is enhanced with a small dish of raspberries sprinkled with a little sugar.

INGREDIENTS

1 pint double cream

1 pint rich or Channel Island milk

1 teaspooon rennet (available in chemists and supermarkets)

3 ozs caster sugar

1 teaspoon ground cinnamon

1 teaspoon rose water

1/4 pint single cream

1 dessertspoon caster sugar

METHOD

Whisk the milk and cream together with the rennet and leave them to form curds and whey (this may take from 20 minutes to 1 1/2 hours depending on how warm and fresh the milk is). When the liquids and solids are clearly separated, strain them through a fine cloth, keeping the curds and discarding the whey. Beat the curds very smoothly - it is possible to do this with an electric beater or a food processor. Add the sugar, rose water, and the cinnamon and stir till smooth. Take a mould with holes in it (many shops still sell these), or a colander lined with a single layer of cheesecloth. Place the cheese in the mould or the colander, smoothing it down, and leave it to set for 1 1/2 hours. Turn it carefully onto an elegant plate and pour 1/4 pint of fine single cream over it before serving. A little sugar to sprinkle on as well is a wonderful accompaniment.

TO MAKE THE ENGLISH FRESH CHEESE

Take a quart of Creame and a quart of new Milke & sett it together with your ordinary runnett when it is Come break the Curd & whey it well, then breake it very small & mingle it with as much sugar as you please & rose water & a little Cinamon & soe mingle all together then put it in a Colander with holes to print it, & an hour and a halfe after turn it into a dish & put Creame to it and soe serve it up

Apricot Souffle

GAMBIER FAMILY, LANGLEY, 1843

Despite its name, this recipe from 1843 is really not a soufflé at all, but an apricot meringue. It comes from the second and later of the cook books that the Gambier family preserved and seems to have been written by the daughter of the author of the Ratafia pudding, qv. The style of the original is much more terse than that of her predecessor but the recipe is delicious nonetheless.

INGREDIENTS

8 ozs sponge cake

1 lb apricot conserve

5 ozs double cream

5 ozs milk

2 tablespoons caster sugar

3 egg whites

METHOD

Break up the sponge cake into pieces about the size of a hazelnut. Cover finely the bottom of a shallow baking dish with the sponge cake. Mix the double cream and milk together and pour it over, allowing 2 or 3 minutes for it to soak into the cake. Spoon the apricot jam evenly over the cake crumbs. Beat the egg whites till they're stiff, add a tablespoonful of the sugar and beat again till glossy, and then fold the remaining tablespoon of sugar in. Place the dish in a preheated low oven, Gas Mark 3, 170 °C, 325 °F until the meringue is set for about an hour, and looks golden in colour.

> ### APRICOT SOUFFLE
> *Four penny Sponge Cakes at the bottom of the Dish broken small (they should be stale) One lb of Apricot Jam spread with the Crumbed Cake - Pour over warm thin cream or rich milk. Beat the Whites of as many eggs as you require for froth. Put it in the Oven to brown.*

A Very Good
Almond Pudding

MARSHAM FAMILY, WHORNES PLACE, 17TH-18TH CENTURY

The British have always been obsessed with almonds. Since the Romans brought them here nearly 2,00[ ] years ago, we've used enormous quantities, though we've very rarely been able to grow them successfu[l]ly in our rather cool climate. In Medieval and Renaissance times they were a staple in the kitchen and th[e] quantity of almond based recipes, particularly puddings, to be found in the archives of the great house[s] testify to the tradition lasting well into the 19th century. Indeed, Bakewell tarts, almond fingers and oth[er] such traditional British baking still maintain their popularity today. The Very Good Almond Pudding [is] very simple and, in fact, represents the basis of almost all of this kind of cooking. This recipe comes fro[m] the late 1600s and the Marsham family, but more than 100 years later the Gambiers at Langley were mal[k]ing what they called a Ratafia pudding, in almost every respect the same except for substituting almon[d] sponge cakes for the ground almonds. The later recipe was a steamed pudding whereas the early on[e] was baked, but there was also a suggestion that it could have been cooked as a pie. So I've taken what [I] think are the best aspects of all the recipes and amalgamated them into a mixture that you can cook o[n] its own, in a pastry case or even as a steamed pudding if you prefer.

INGREDIENTS

1/2 pint each single cream and milk

Grated rind of 1 lemon

1 blade of mace

1 piece of cinnamon stick

3 ozs caster sugar

6 ozs white breadcrumbs

1/4 lb ground almonds
1/4 lb almond biscuits, broken into small pieces
(or 1/2 lb of either almonds or biscuits)

4 eggs

1/2 teaspoon grated nutmeg

1 oz butter

Pinch of salt

ALTERNATIVE 1:

8 ozs shortcrust pastry

ALTERNATIVE 2:

1-2 tablespoons candied peel

1-2 tablespoons currants

METHOD

Bring the milk and cream to the boil, add the mace, cinnamon, lemon rind and sugar, stir well and simmer for 10 minutes. In a mixing bowl, place the breadcrumbs and the almond biscuits. Pour in the milk mixture through a sieve a[nd] stir in the ground almonds. Mix thoroughly. Beat the eggs until foamy, add the nutmeg and salt, and mix with the mil[k] and almond mixture when it has cooled to below blood he[at]. Either butter a gratin dish, pour the mixture in and bake it i[n] a preheated oven at Gas Mark 5, 190,°C 375 °F for about 45 minutes.

Alternatively line an 8 inch pie tin with shortcrust pastry an[d] pour the mixture into that, baking it at the same temperatur[e] but for about 5 to 10 minutes longer.

The last alternative is to butter a pudding basin, pour the m[ix]ture into that, adding a tablespoon or two of candied peel and currants. Cover with a pleated piece of greaseproof pap[er] and place in a saucepan with 3 inches of water around it. Simmer for 1 3/4 hours before turning it out.

Pets

LADY RACHEL FANE, KNOLE, 1630

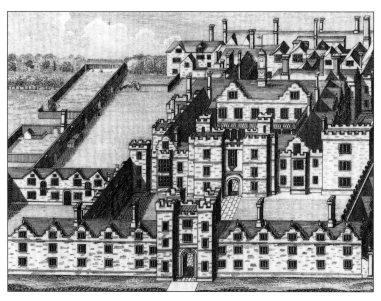

Lady Rachel Fane, who wrote this recipe down in 1630, lived at Knole. She was a member of the Sackville family, which had been given the house lease by Elizabeth I. What is particularly interesting about this recipe is that it is clearly a recipe for meringues which, common wisdom has it, did not make a formal appearance in cookery until the end of the 17th century, nearly 70 years later. But that view comes from the French history of cooking and as Hilary Spurling remarks in her book about Lady Eleanor Fettiplace, a contemporary of Lady Rachel Fane, "Clearly Lady Fettiplace did not invent ordinary meringues but she indisputably made and ate them well before they are generally thought to have been invented at all".

This recipe, very simply, creates delicate individual meringues. The recipe is clearly a personal one, because of the addendum at the end suggesting the inclusion of musk and ambergris. (Two extremely expensive animal based resins from the musk deer and the sperm whale respectively.) Neither is obtainable very easily these days and, indeed, the sperm whale is quite rightly protected, so I suggest the use of a little ground aniseed, which Lady Fettiplace used in her version of these biscuits.

You may not want to use a candle to check them with, but it's certainly a good idea to follow the advice of placing a shallow bowl of water in the oven to ensure they don't cook too fast.

They are wonderful with the fruit creams to be found on pages 94 and 95

LADY RACHEL FANE

Lady Rachel Fane was a relation of the Sackvilles - heirs of Thomas Sackville who was the first Earl of Dorset and Lord Treasurer under both Elizabeth I and James I. Though they continued to move in high circles, the later Sackvilles had rather more frivolous tastes, as demonstrated by the life-size nude statue of the Italian mistress of the Third Duke, still to be seen in the house. Lady Rachel herself was a vivid personality. Apart from her recipe book and manuscript of a masque performed by her children in 1625, the most poignant of her mementoes is a hand-drawn and coloured playing card of the Queen of Diamonds marked 'Rachel'.

INGREDIENTS	*METHOD*
6 egg whites	Beat the egg whites until they are really stiff and then add all but 2 tablespoons of the sugar, a spoonful at a time beating as you go until the meringue is glossy. Mix the coriander and aniseed with the remaining sugar, crushing it gently, and fold it carefully into the meringue. Take a large baking sheet and lightly butter it, or spread it with a sheet of nonstick baking parchment. Place a tablespoon of the meringue onto the surface , leaving at least half an inch around each one for spreading. Bake in a very low preheated oven Gas Mark 1, 140 °C, 275 °F or a plate warming Aga oven and cook for 1 to 1½ hours. They're really meant to dry out rather than bake and should remain white throughout. Allow them to cool before lifting off. They will store in a tin for 3 to 4 days if it's airtight.

½ lb caster sugar

1 oz butter

1 teaspoon lightly crushed coriander seeds

1 teaspoon lightly crushed aniseeds

TO MAKE PETS

Take a pownd of Drye fine searsed suger, & beat the whites very wel then take off the froutgh & put your suger, bye litle & litle in to it - contineually stiring it & beating it with a spoone ore laydle, & when it is exceedingly well beaten, then have some pye plates ready buttred & wipe the buter of because the lesse buter it hath the beter, then drope them upon the plate & put in to every drope a carieway seede or coriander then let your oven be very temparate & watch them with a candle all the while & if they be right they will rise & looke very white, it is good at the first to set a scilet of water, with them in to the oven, & when they be thowrow drye then take them out, you must in the mixing of them put 12 graines of muske & 12 of Aber grisse which you must bruse with suger before you stire it in to the egge & suger

KNOLE

Knole is one of Britain's greatest houses. Originally built by Thomas Bouchier, Archbishop of Canterbury in the 15th century, it was taken from the Archbishops by Henry VIII and passed, in Elizabeth's reign, to the Sackville family whose descendants still live there. The house is the size of an Oxford college and is reputed to have seven courtyards for the days of the week, 52 staircases for the weeks of the year, and 365 rooms. Visitors often remark on the palpable feeling of history frozen in time in this extraordinary building set in 1,000 acres of parkland and gardens.

Sparkling Gooseberry Wine

GAMBIER FAMILY, LANGLEY, 1808

English Champagne

To every [...] picked [...]
bruised, add [...] them sla[...]
in a tub 3 [...] ry day —
every gallon [...] d (that is
pressed by [...] cloth and a
standing a lit [...] ed off from
settling) put [...] Barrel it u
dd a bottle of [...] 20 quarts o
quor. Bring [...] prish and a
nd of 3 Weeks [...] the propos
I ½ an oun [...] ously dissol
n some of the liquor with a stick introdu
into the bunghole stir the whole well togethe
nce a day, in a little time afterwards it may be
unged down close — the gooseberries mus
ull grown but must not have begun to tur

From the quantities involved, the Gambier family, whose recipe this is, seem to have been very fond of the result. The Reverend J.E. Gambier was rector of St. Mary's in the village of Langley which backs onto the Leeds Castle estate in central Kent. At the end of the 18th and the beginning of the 19th century he may well have used the gallons of wine as an economic basis for parish hospitality and entertaining. The quantities I suggest, should make half a dozen bottles, enough to establish if you have a taste for the vintage.

INGREDIENTS

5 lbs firm, ripe gooseberries

1 gallon of water, boiled and allowed to cool

3½ lbs sugar

¼ bottle Grappa or similar white grape spirit, such as Eau de Vie de Marc

½ teaspoon gelatine or agar agar, stirred into a little water and allowed to soak

(Large sealed container with an air vent system available from home brewing shops)

METHOD

Wash and lightly crush the gooseberries so that they give out some juice. Place them in a wooden, glass or earthenware container and pour over the water. Leave to stand for 3 days. Strain through a cheesecloth, squeezing the pulp to get all the juice out. Allow to stand for 6 hours before pouring off the clear liquids, leaving the detrius at the bottom of the container. Stir in the sugar until dissolved and place in the large sealed container. Allow to work for 3 days, add the Grappa or Marc and, after 2 weeks more, add the gelatine. Stir it thoroughly with a stick or glass rod daily for a week and then bottle, making sure that the corks are well strapped down. It needs 3 to 6 months in a cool dark place before consumption.

SPARKLING GOOSEBERRY WINE

To every lb of gooseberries, when picked & bruised, add one quart of Water let them stand in a tub 3 days stirring them every day - to every gallon of juice when strained (that is pressed by the hand through a coarse cloth and after standing a little time carefully poured off from the settling) put 3 lbs of good loaf sugar. Barrel it and add a bottle of white Brandy to every 20 quarts of liquor. Bung the cask down lightly at first and at the end of 3 weeks add some Isinglass in the proportion of ½ an ounce to ten gallons previously dissolved in some of the liquor & with a stick introduced into the bunghole stire the whole well together once a day, in a little time afterwards it may be bunged down close - the gooseberries must be full grown but must not have begun to turn

---

THE GAMBIER FAMILY

The Gambiers were a family deeply involved with the Anglican church. The two cookery books from 1808 and 1843 were probably the work of the wife and daughter of the Reverend J.E Gambier, who was Rector at Langley in central Kent for nearly 40 years. The family was closely related to the Venns, who were, throughout the 19th century, well-known Evangelical divines, and one later member of the family went on to become an Admiral of the fleet, while others married into various parts of the aristocracy. The family had an extraordinarily wide range of interests visible in the archives, which contain naturalist pocket books with illustrations of insects and plants, poems, medical compilations, as well as the cookery books.

Barley Water

FILMER FAMILY, EAST SUTTON PLACE, EARLY 19TH CENTURY

This is a very simple recipe for a home-made drink that we still have in a commercial version. It used to be made at harvest time, late July and August, in huge quantities as an extremely refreshing drink for the people reaping by hand - an arduous and dusty occupation. The barley in the water of course gave strength as well as flavour to the drink. I've included in the modern version some sugar, because we're used to sweetened drinks. It's worth trying it in the original form if you want a really astringent refreshing taste, as it might have been drunk in the fields of the Filmer family around East Sutton Place when Napoleon still ruled in France. It's sufficiently strong to be diluted a little if you wish.

G. Scharf.

INGREDIENTS

3 ozs pearl barley

2 pints boiling water

Grated rind and juice of 1 lemon

6 tablespoons sugar

METHOD

Place the pearl barley in a jug and pour over the water. Add the lemon rind and lemon juice and sugar and stir thoroughly. Allow to cool. Strain into a clean jug or bottle before using.

THE FILMER FAMILY

The Filmer family lived originally at Otterden and moved to East Sutton in the reign of the first Elizabeth. The family married into the local gentry and supported Charles during the Civil War. They went on to prosper in the 18th and early 19th century with the interesting reputation of producing huge families. Two Sir Edward Filmers in the 17th and 18th century had families of 18 and 20 children each respectively. The last Baronet, Sir Robert, was killed early in the First World War. The cookery book, by an unknown hand is from the early 19th Century.

EAST SUTTON PLACE

East Sutton Place is now a borstal institution, but from the middle of the 16th century until into the 20th it was the home of the Filmer family. With its red brick spaciousness, it has seen Elizabeth I's judges, an attack by Fairfax's troops during the Civil war (the bullet holes are still there), famous authors, and it regularly housed families of more than 18 children. Today, of course, the house cannot be visited but the Church carries many memorials to the departed family

SPRING   SUMMER.

AUTUMN   WINTER

OF 1860.

BARLEY-WATER
3 Table-spoonful of Pearl-barly, to be washed clean, add to it a quart of boiling water & half the rind of a good Lemon, let it stand until cold

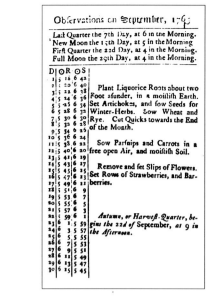

Obſervations on September, 1765.

Laſt Quarter the 7th Day, at 6 in the Morning.
New Moon the 15th Day, at 5 in the Morning
Firſt Quarter the 22d Day, at 4 in the Morning.
Full Moon the 29th Day, at 4 in the Morning.

D	⊙ R	⊙ S	
1	5 18	6 42	
2	5 20	6 40	Plant Liquorice Roots about two
3	5 22	6 38	Foot aſunder, in a moiſtiſh Earth.
4	5 24	6 36	Set Artichokes, and ſow Seeds for
5	5 26	6 34	Winter-Herbs. Sow Wheat and
6	5 28	6 32	Rye. Cut Quicks towards the End
7	5 30	6 30	of the Month.
8	5 32	6 28	
9	5 34	6 25	
10	5 36	6 24	
11	5 38	6 22	Sow Parſnips and Carrots in a
12	5 40	6 20	free open Air, and moiſtiſh Soil.
13	5 41	6 19	
14	5 43	6 17	Remove and ſet Slips of Flowers.
15	5 45	6 15	Set Rows of Strawberries, and Bar-
16	5 47	6 13	berries.
17	5 49	6 11	
18	5 51	6 9	
19	5 53	6 7	
20	5 55	6 5	
21	5 57	6 3	
22	5 59	6 1	Autumn, or Harveſt-Quarter, be-
23	6 1	5 59	gins the 22d of September, at 9 in
24	6 3	5 57	the Afternoon.
25	6 5	5 55	
26	6 7	5 53	
27	6 9	5 51	
28	6 11	5 49	
29	6 13	5 47	
30	6 15	5 45	

If Summer was a time of celebration in the Britain of the 17th and 18th centuries, Autumn was the time of plenty. It was also the time of the hardest work. The corn, hopefully, was in, whether it was wheat, barley or oats, but now the orchards' produce needed storing or drying. By the end of November the hens would be ceasing to lay, but their eggs needed to be preserved to last through until the end of Spring. Vegetables needed to be salted or pickled as well as being enjoyed fresh at the time. Herbs needed drying and fruit needed turning into jams and conserves, drinks and medicines. Towards the end of the season, just before Christmas there would be the slaughtering of the animals that couldn't be fed through the Winter. It was only at the end of the 18th century that new agricultural techniques and early forms of silage began to change the pattern. So, there was meat to be salted and turned into patés and hams, and there was much feasting too on the by-products and surpluses of the time. It was also a season for game, much more plentiful in the countryside then than it is now, although often reserved for the owners of the land with harsh punishments for others who sought to help themselves. Autumn too, as many of the little inserts show, was a time when medicines and nostrums were being laid by for the long, cold and dark days to come.

Obſervations on October, 1765.

Laſt Quarter the 7th Day, at 1 in the Morning.
New Moon the 14th Day, at 5 in the Afternoon.
Firſt Quarter the 21ſt Day, at 11 in the Morning.
Full Moon the 28th Day, at 6 in the Afternoon.

D	⊙ R	⊙ S	
1	6 17	5 43	Tranſplant your brown Dutch
2	6 19	5 41	and common Letuces upon warm
3	6 21	5 39	Borders, to abide the Winter; ſow
4	6 23	5 37	all Sorts of Sallad-Herbs upon de-
5	6 25	5 35	cay'd Hot-Beds, ſuch as Letuce,
6	6 27	5 33	Creſſes, Radiſh, Muſtard, and Spi-
7	6 29	5 31	nage Earth up Sellery, Chardoons,
8	6 31	5 29	and the Stems of Broccoli Plants, to
9	6 32	5 28	protect them from the Froſt.
10	6 34	5 26	
11	6 36	5 24	Make Plantations of the Suckers
12	6 38	5 22	of Gooſberries, Currants, and Raſ-
13	6 40	5 20	berries. Cut Artichokes with long
14	6 42	5 18	Stalks, which you may preſerve in
15	6 44	5 16	the Houſe, by ſetting them in Sand.
16	6 46	5 14	
17	6 48	5 12	Continue to ſow Wheat, ſet up
18	6 50	5 10	your Barley Land, ſow Maſts for
19	6 52	5 8	Coppices or Hedge-Rows; plant
20	6 54	5 6	Quick-Sets and plaſh Hedges; and
21	6 56	5 4	plant all Sorts of Foreſt-Trees that
22	6 58	5 2	ſhed their Leaves.
23	7 0	5 0	
24	7 2	4 58	Avoid being out late at Nights,
25	7 4	4 56	or in foggy Weather; for a Cold
26	7 6	4 54	now got, may continue the whole
27	7 8	4 52	Winter.
28	7 9	4 51	
29	7 11	4 49	
30	7 13	4 47	
31	7 14	4 46	

Obſervations on November, 1765.

Laſt Quarter the 5th Day, at 9 at Night.
New Moon the 13th Day, at 4 in the Morning.
Firſt Quarter the 19th Day, at 7 at Night.
Full Moon the 27th Day, at 11 in the Morning.

D	⊙ R	⊙ S	
1	7 16	4 44	If the Seaſon prove mild, you
2	7 18	4 42	may continue to prune Apple-Trees,
3	7 20	4 40	be they Standards, Wall-Fruit, or
4	7 21	4 39	Eſpaliers; but you ſhould not prune
5	7 23	4 37	them later, leſt Rains and Froſts
6	7 25	4 35	ſhould hurt the Trees, when the
7	7 27	4 33	Wounds are freſh.
8	7 29	4 31	
9	7 30	4 30	
10	7 32	4 28	
11	7 34	4 26	Trench your Ground, by laying
12	7 36	4 24	it up in Ridges to mellow. Set
13	7 37	4 23	Crab-Tree Stocks to graft on; con-
14	7 39	4 21	tinue to plant Suckers and Cuttings
15	7 40	4 20	of Gooſberries, Currants, and Raſ-
16	7 42	4 18	berries; make Hot-Beds for Aſpa-
17	7 44	4 16	ragus; fell Coppices, and lop Trees;
18	7 45	4 15	plant Timber and Fruit-Trees, if
19	7 46	4 14	the Weather be open.
20	7 48	4 12	
21	7 49	4 11	
22	7 50	4 10	
23	7 52	4 8	The beſt Phyſick this Month is
24	7 53	4 7	good Exerciſe, warm Clothes, and
25	7 54	4 6	wholeſome Diet: But if any Diſ-
26	7 56	4 4	temper afflict you, finiſh your Phy-
27	7 57	4 3	ſick this Month, and ſo reſt till
28	7 59	4 1	March.
29	8 0	4 0	
30	8 1	3 59	

autumn

Vegetable Soup

GAMBIER FAMILY, LANGLEY, 1843

This is a classic Rectory soup - simple, nutritious and using the produce available to the Gambier family from their own gardens. Made in these sort of quantities it must have been intended to feed more than the household. *You* could keep it in the fridge, but it is more likely to have been eaten at some kind of parish occasion. A modern version, made in smaller quantities, makes a marvellous first course for a weekend family lunch.

INGREDIENTS

½lb each fresh turnips, carrots, potatoes, onions, peeled and diced into half inch cubes

½ lb celery, trimmed and diced

2 ozs butter

1 oz olive oil

2 pints water

Salt and Pepper

1 tablespoon parsley or celery leaves. chopped

METHOD

Melt the butter in the oil and fry the vegetables gently for about 5 minutes. Season generously, add the water and simmer for 25 to 30 minutes. Place in a liquidiser or food processor and process until as smooth as possible. A tablespoon of parsley or celery leaves, finely chopped and stirred in after processing, is an attractive addition.

VEGETABLE SOUP (VERY GOOD)
Six turnips, the same of carrots, potatoes onions & heads of celery sliced & fried in butter - Six quarts of water Stew six hours rub thro' a seive Season it to taste. Make hot & it is ready for table -

A Very Pretty Dish of Eggs

UNKNOWN, 1818

This is a very cottagey recipe, simple, inexpensive and made from totally local ingredients. It's nevertheless extremely delicious and, made in individual ramekin dishes, is a splendid first course. In larger quantities it also makes a nice light lunch. I suggest you serve it with wholemeal toast or crisp french bread.

INGREDIENTS

4 large eggs

2 tablespoons melted butter

2 tablespoons white breadcrumbs

2 tablespoons parsley, chopped

Salt and Pepper

4 ramekin dishes or a large baking dish

METHOD

Use a little of the butter to grease the ramekin dishes or the larger baking dish. Break the eggs into a cup and add to the ramekin dishes or larger baking dish. Pour a little butter over each one and sprinkle the breadcrumbs over the top. Place them in a hot oven, Gas Mark 6, 200 °C, 400 °F for 6 to 8 minutes until the yolks have veiled over and the whites are set. Sprinkle generously with parsley and season for serving.

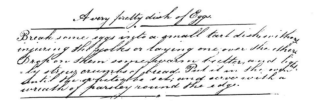

A VERY PRETTY DISH OF EGGS
Break some eggs into a small tart dish, without injuring the yolks or laying one over the other. Drop on them some warm butter and lightly strew crumbs of bread. Put it in the oven until the whites be set; and serve with a wreath of parsley round the edge

Oyster Loves

MARSHAM FAMILY, WHORNES PLACE, 17TH-18TH CENTURY

The North Kent coast has been famous for oysters since Roman times. Recently pollution and disease has almost wiped out the native oysters, both in Kent and on the beds further north in the Colchester area of Essex, where they've been replaced by Pacific varieties. But in the 1650s, when this recipe was noted down by the Marsham family, living at that time at Cuxton on the Medway, from their Dering cousin living at Pluckley, oysters were the food of the poor, sold by the barrel-load, they were so plentiful. This was a method of cooking them and presenting them in what were known as Coffyns - an obvious reference to the shape of these small baked containers fashioned from bread. With oysters being a little more of a luxury item these days, I've reduced the quantity slightly. The dish is different, but still delicious made with mussels. The bread containers are a marvellous idea and can be filled with all kinds of other ingredients like ratatouille or flavoured scrambled eggs if mussels or oysters are not to your taste.

INGREDIENTS

2 short French loaves (about 12 to 14 inches long)

24 oysters, shelled or 2 pints of mussels

1 tablespoon onion, finely chopped

1 teaspoon fresh thyme, chopped

1 pinch each of ground cloves, mace and black pepper

1 teaspoon lemon juice

2 egg yolks

5 ozs butter, melted

Liquid from oysters / 1/4 pint water for the mussels

2 tablespoons parsley, chopped

METHOD 1 USING OYSTERS

Place the oysters with any liquid you've managed to save in a saucepan. Add the lemon juice and simmer for 5 minutes. Then add the parsley, onion, thyme and the spices. Cut each loaf in half and trim the ends. Cut a lid off a quarter of an inch thick. Scoop out the bread from the four bases leaving a half inch wall all round in each base. Keep the scooped out bread. Brush the four bases and lids with the butter thoroughly. Bake in a Gas Mark 4, 180 °C, 350 °F oven for 10 minutes until lightly brown and crisp. In the meantime take 4 tablespoons of the bread and add it to the fish and its juices. Stir the egg yolks into the remaining butter and mix into the fish. Stir gently until it has amalgamated and thickened. Do not let it boil or it will curdle. Spoon the oysters in their sauce into the prepared containers, sprinkle with a little more fresh parsley and arrange with the lid on when serving.

METHOD 2 USING MUSSELS

Scrub the mussels making sure that they're neither open nor broken. Place them in a saucepan with a lid with 1/4 pint of water. Add the lemon juice and put them over a high heat until they've opened. Take out the mussels, discard the shells and strain the liquid. Place the mussels and liquid back in the saucepan, adding one tablespoon of chopped parsley, the onion, thyme and spices. Cut each loaf in half and trim the ends. Cut a lid off a quarter of an inch thick. Scoop out the bread from the four bases, leaving a half inch wall all round in each base. Keep the scooped out bread. Brush the four bases and lids with the butter thoroughly. Bake in a preheated Gas Mark 4, 180 °C, 350 °F oven for 10 minutes until lightly brown and crisp. In the meantime take 4 tablespoons of the bread and add it to the fish and its juices. Stir the egg yolks into the remaining butter and mix into the fish. Stir gently until it has all amalgamated and thickened. Do not let it boil or it will curdle. Spoon the mussels in their sauce into the prepared containers, sprinkle with a little more fresh parsley and arrange with the lid on when serving.

COSEN DERING OYSTER LOVES

Take 3 pints of oysters to 4 French roles stew the(e)m a little in thaire owne Liquor. straine the(e)m of &
pick th(e)m well th(e)n put th(e)m into a sauce pan w(i)th a little parsley a little time a little onion
minced altogether a little cloves & mace & a little pepper a little of the oyster Liquor a quarter of a pint
of whit wine & a slice of lemmon put it over the fier & stew it together put a little grated bread to it beat
2 or 3 yelks of egges w(i)th a little butter w(hi)ch thicken it cut a hole on the top of y(ou)r bread & take
out the crumb th(e)n take Clarrified butter enough to them w(hi)ch will be 3 pound scalding hott put
th(e)m in & turne th(e)m let th(e)m be crispe but not browne th(e)n have the oysters ready hott to put
in cover th(e)m w(i)th the covers you took of the bread & sarve th(e)m so in.

An Oyster Shell

A. Lady's Bonnet.

THE MARSHAM FAMILY

The Marsham family lived, from the end of the 16th century, at Whornes Place at Cuxton on the Medway. The family has a formidable scholarly reputation with two Sir John Marshams, father and son concentrating on ancient and English history. It is likely that the recipe book containing both culinary and medicinal recipes collected in the 17th and early 18th century was principally the work of the second Sir John Marsham. In the 18th century the family moved from Cuxton to The Mote at Maidstone and one or two recipes towards the end of the collection record this move in the naming of dishes.

To Fricafsee Turbut

MRS WOLFE, WESTERHAM, 18TH CENTURY

Fricassee in this context means frying and this is a luscious recipe for an expensive fish. The turbot specified is the grand kind of flat fish that's occasionally still to be found in good fishmongers. You may want to try this recipe with a slightly cheaper fish such as hake or large haddock or, perhaps best of all, although not much cheaper than turbot, halibut. Either way the fish is made to go quite a lot further with the force meat balls - a tradition that seems to have died completely in the last hundred years but was often used to both add quantity and flavour to expensive foods in the past. Mrs Wolfe, who collected this recipe in the mid-18th century, would of course have had access even in inland Westerham to plenty of cheap oysters to help extend it as well. If you want something of the sort without the expense that current day oysters provide, try using the widely available New Zealand green lip mussels fried for 2 or 3 minutes in a little foaming butter with a 1/4 lb of button mushrooms. New or mashed potatoes are excellent with this dish.

INGREDIENTS

1 1/2 lbs turbot or other fish (see above), filleted and skinned

1 egg

1/4 lb rich milk

2 tablespoons flour

1/4 teaspoon grated nutmeg

Sunflower oil - amount depends on method of cooking fish

FOR THE FISH SAUCE:

Fish trimmings, skin, bones etc.

Grated rind and juice of half a lemon

12 fl ozs water

4 tablespoons cream

1 dessertspoon cornflour mixed with a little water

1 dessertspoon butter

FOR THE FORCEMEAT BALLS:

6 ozs soft white breadcrumbs

2 tablespoons parsley, chopped

1 egg

1 tablespoon butter (or the more traditional suet)

Salt and Pepper

TO GARNISH:

1 tablespoon parsley, chopped

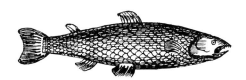

TO FRICAFSEE TURBUT

Take a Turbut, cut in short slices without ye skin. Make a little Batter to dip it in, of Eggs cream a little flower a little mace & nutmeg. Then fry it a fine Brown, make a few forst meat balls & some good fish sauce to serve it up in, with fried Oysters mushrooms etc. round it.

METHOD

FOR THE FISH SAUCE:

Place the fish trimmings, lemon rind and lemon juice in the water. Bring to a fast boil for 10 minutes and strain. Stir in the cream and cornflour. Add the butter and simmer gently till well thickened.

FOR THE FISH:

Cut the turbot in one inch slices. Beat the egg into the milk, stir in the flour and the nutmeg. Dip the fish in the batter and either deep fry for 4 to 5 minutes in clean oil or shallow fry 3 minutes a side in a 1/2 inch of oil in a nonstick frying pan.

FOR THE FORCEMEAT BALLS:

Mix all the the ingredients together and knead till coherent. Divide into 12 small portions, roll them into balls and fry with the fish for 3 to 4 minutes until lightly browned.

TO SERVE:

Place the fish pieces along an oval platter, surround with the forcemeat balls and the fried oysters or mussels and mushrooms if being used. Place a thin line of sauce up the centre, sprinkle with a little parsley and serve the remaining sauce separately.

To Boyl a Carp ye French Way

MRS WOLFE, WESTERHAM, 18TH CENTURY

Carp, which these days seems a very specialised fish, was except on the sea coast, the most widely avail able fish anywhere in Britain for centuries. This was because it was the first successfully farmed fish, and the great Abbey and Manorial fish ponds, some of which still exist (although they're not often used for fish farming these days), were stocked with carp. The big rivers also had wild carp in them and many of the big French rivers like the Loire still do. Carp is available today from most fishmongers. If you fancy trying the recipe but not the fish itself, which can sometimes have a slightly muddy texture and taste, the recipe works very well with our own farmed trout or small salmon. It should be served with a watercress and orange salad and some home-made mayonnaise.

INGREDIENTS

2 tablespoons lemon juice

2 pints water

1 bouquet garni of 'sweet herbs', parsley, a sprig of thyme, a stick of celery and a sprig of fennel

Pinch of salt

2 cloves

6 peppercorns

1 x 2-2½ lb fish - carp, salmon or trout

2 oz butter, softened

2 large Spanish onions, peeled and finely sliced

¼ pint cider vinegar

Salt and Pepper

METHOD

Mix the lemon juice and the water together. Add the onions, the bouquet garni, the salt, cloves and peppercorns and bring to the boil. Simmer for 10 minutes. Season the cavity of the fish generously with salt and pepper, and place the butter inside. Lower the fish into the hot liquid and simmer for 5 minutes per lb. Switch the heat off and pour in the cider vinegar. Let the fish lie in the water till cool. Remove carefully to a serving dish. It can be chilled gently in the refrigerator for up to 24 hours.
(N.B. If a larger carp is used, the volume of liquids needs to be increased by 50-100%.)

Harico of Mutton

WOODGATE FAMILY, CHIDDINGSTONE, 1765

We think haricot are the little white French beans so widely popularised in French recipes like the famous Cassoulet, but in fact the Oxford dictionary defines haricot as a ragout or stew usually of mutton, and lamb, the beans natural companions as butter is to bread. You might like to serve this Autumn version of a Navarin-like stew with some haricot beans. If you want to use fresh chestnuts in the recipe, cut a little slit in the skin of each nut, dip them in boiling water for 30 seconds, and peel the skin off while they're still as hot as you can handle them. This dish could also be served with lots of mashed potato.

HARICOT BEANS

1/2 lb beans soaked for 6 hours, boiled and then simmered for a couple of hours with a finely, chopped onion and some herbs, drained and mixed with a little of the juices from the stew.

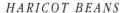

INGREDIENTS

6 chump chops of lamb or mutton

1 tablespoon oil

8 ozs each turnips and carrots, peeled and cut into half inch die

24 chestnuts peeled (as above) or dried chestnuts soaked in warm water for 30 minutes

2 little gem lettuces, washed and cut into rounds half an inch thick

6 small pickling style onions, peeled

1 sprig each of thyme, celery and parsley, chopped

1 blade of mace

1 tablespoon plain flour

1 breakfast cup of water

METHOD

Lightly flour the chump chops and fry until lightly browned on both sides in the oil in a large frying pan. Pour out the fat, put in the turnips and carrots, the chestnuts, the lettuces the onions and the herbs. Season generously, add the blade of mace and water. Give the pan a shake and cover closely using foil if the lid isn't too well fitting. Let it cook over a low heat - an asbestos mat is useful - for 40 to 45 minutes c 1 hour if using mutton chops. Serve on deep plates.

A HARICO OF MUTTON
Take a Neck or loin of Mutton, cut it into six pieces flour it & fry it brown on both sides in the stew pan, th(e)n pour out all the fat, put in some Turnips & Carrots Cut like dice 2 dozen of chestnuts blanched 2 or 3 lettuces cut small 6 little round Onions a bundle (of sweet herbs?) some pepper & salt & 2 or 3 blades of Mace. Cover it Close & let it stew for an Hour take of the fat & dish it up.

Ox or Calves Tails

POLHILL FAMILY, CHIPSTEAD HOUSE, EARLY 19TH CENTURY

Calves tails aren't very easily come by these days but the recipe is very good with the larger and meaty oxtail. The thing about oxtail is that there is a lot more bone than meat to each slice so although the flavour and texture of the dish is always terrific, they're not the easiest things in the world to eat. This recipe, interestingly, uses a technique often found in France whereby the meat is cooked until it's easy to remove from the bone and this is done before the dish is served. It makes for much more elegant presentation and consumption. Allspice, by the way, is a pepper-like spice imported from Jamaica, the pearl of British colonies in the 18th and early 19th centuries, and is native to that country. It has a flavour reminiscent of a mixture of cinnamon and nutmeg.

Serve with lots of mashed potato, carrots and crisp cabbage or sprouts.

INGREDIENTS

2 1/2 lbs oxtail, sectioned

1 large onion, peeled and stuck with 3 cloves

5 peppercorns

5 allspice berries

1 teaspoon salt

1 tablespoon each butter and flour, mashed together

1 tablespoon parsley, chopped

METHOD

Place the oxtail pieces into a saucepan, cover them with cold water and bring them to the boil. Skim the surface with a wooden spoon of any froth and then put in the onion, peppercorns allspice and teaspoon of salt. Cover the saucepan and let it cook very gently for about 1 1/2 to 2 hours. It can also be placed in a preheated medium oven Gas Mark 4, 180 °C, 350 °F with less danger of it burning. Allow the stew to cool. If it can be left in the fridge over night all the fat will rise to the surface and can be easily removed. Take the meat off the bone by hand (it should be very easy to do) and strain the sauce. Reheat the sauce, stirring in the butter and flour. This will thicken the sauce. Add the meat and reheat. Sprinkle with parsley before serving.

OX OR CALVES TAILS STEWED

Divide at each joint the ox or calf's tail - wash them well - put them in a saucepan - just cover them with cold water & set them on the fire - When they boil take off the skum & put in an onion - 3 cloves or two blades of Mace - a few berries of black pepper - the same of Allspice, & 1/2 a teaspoonsful of salt - cover the stewpan close & let it simmer very gently till the tails are quite tender - this will take from one hour & a 1/2 to two hours & a 1/2 - Take out the bones & thicken the gravy with a little flour & butter - serve up quite hot.

Beef Steak Pudding

DELELAH TYLER, 1840

One of the great classics of English cookery, in this version is very economically produced. Mrs Delelah Tyler, who noted it down in the 1840s in her personal cookery book, had quite grand ambitions. Related to the Roper family, the descendants of Henry VIII's Chancellor, Sir Thomas More, she sought and obtained a grant of a coat of arms in 1835 but clearly had a strong sense of domestic economy to go with her aspirations. There's nothing wrong with this pudding for all that. There's plenty of meat to vegetables and if you fancy something a little richer you could always add 1/2 lb of lambs kidneys or button mushrooms. You could add, if you were feeling extravagant, half a dozen oysters. All would be traditional, but I think this recipe is worth trying in its original form, generously flavoured as it is. The cloth in the original is a method of simply removing the hot basin easily. A long strip of folded foil placed in the saucepan under the basin with its end hanging out both sides is a modern way of achieving the same process. Boiled potatoes and plenty of lightly cooked cabbage would be perfect accompaniments. It will serve at least six.

INGREDIENTS

FOR THE SUET PASTRY:

1/2 lb beef suet

1 1/4 lb flour

Pinch of salt

1/2 pint milk and water mixed

METHOD

Mix the suet, flour and salt together, before adding the liquid. A food processor may be used and saves on the rolling pin.

FOR THE FILLING:

2 lbs beef steak (stewing is fine), trimmed of fat and cut into cubes

1 large onion, peeled and chopped

1 lb peeled waxy potatoes (desiree or other similar)

Salt and Pepper

1/2 teaspoon grated nutmeg

1 tablespoon Worcestershire sauce

1 tablespoon lemon pickle or the grated rind and juice of 1 lemon

1 dessertspoon butter or oil

METHOD

Slice the potatoes once lengthwise and then into slices 1/4 of an inch thick. Take a 2 pint pudding basin, lightly oil or butter it, roll out 3/4 of the pastry and use it to line the basin. Put a layer of steak pieces in, season generously with salt, pepper and nutmeg, sprinkle on a third of the onion, then half of the potatoes, another layer of steak, seasoned and sprinkled, a layer of onions and the rest of the potatoes and finish with a last layer of steak with onion and seasoning. Mix the Worcestershire sauce, lemon pickle or rind and juice of the lemon and pour them over the meat and potato mixture. The liquid should come to half an inch short of the basin, so if necessary, top it up with water. Roll out the top and close the basin off with it, making sure the seal is complete. Cover with pleated grease proof paper, tied down. Place in a large saucepan with 4 inches of boiling water. Cover it and boil for 2 1/2 hours. When it is out of the saucepan, put a plate upside down on the top and turn the whole lot over carefully, allowing the pudding to slide out. Before removing the basin, tip any loose moisture off the plate and then take the basin away and serve.

a capital story –
"not to be repeated"

BEEF STEAK PUDDING
Get rump steaks, not too thick, beat them with a chopper, cut them into pieces about half the size of your hand and trim off all the skin, sinews & have ready an onion peeled and chopped fine, likewise some Potatoes peeled and cut into slices a quarter of an inch thick rub the inside of a basin or an oval plain mould shut it with Paste as directed for boiling Puddings season the Steaks with Pepper Salt, and a little grated Nutmeg: put in a layer of Steak, then another of Potatoes and so on till it is full ocasionally throwing in part of the chopped onion: add to it half a gill of Mushroom Catsup a little spoonful of Lemon pickle, and half a gill of water or veal broth, roll out a top and close it well to prevent the water getting in rinse a clean cloth in hot water, sprinkle a little flour over it & tie up the Pudding have ready a large pot of water boiling put it in, and boil it two hours and a half take it up remove the cloth, turn it downwards in a deep dish, and when waisted take away the bain or mould
(Paste for Boiled puddings
Pick and chop very fine half pound of Beef Suet, add to it one pound and a quarter of Flour and a little salt mix it with half a pint of milk or water, and beat it well with the roling pin to incorporate the suet with the flour -)

To Jug a Hare

FILMER FAMILY, EAST SUTTON PLACE, EARLY 19TH CENTURY

There are a number of hare recipes, not surprisingly, in the cookery collections of the 18th and 19th centuries. Hares were particularly plentiful at Harvest time, large numbers of them were captured from the small pocket of standing corn left in the middle of the field as the scythemen worked their way through it. Hare were also hunted, sometimes with greyhounds at other times than Harvest. The most popular way of cooking this country treat was undoubtedly jugging, though there are recipes for more continental styles of cookery. One of these noted down by Delelah Tyler in 1840 was obviously so delicious that she recommended "that you eat as much of it as you can". My favourite version though comes from the Filmer family at East Sutton Place, whose extensive grounds would have provided plenty of the raw material. It's a very simple recipe, but works extremely well with the rich dark meat that hare provides. Get your butcher or game dealer to skin it and cut it into serving pieces. Boiled potatoes, carrots and crisp cooked red or green cabbage are a wonderful accompaniment.

INGREDIENTS

1 hare, sectioned

1 blade of mace, crushed in a mortar

1 bundle of herbs, parsley, thyme, celery and bay leaf

1 glass of red wine or cranberry juice

2 anchovy fillets

2 onions, peeled and each stuck with 2 cloves

1 pinch of ground cloves, mace and cayenne pepper

1 tablespoon each redcurrant jelly and made mustard

1 dessertspoon cornflour mixed with a little water

Salt and Pepper

METHOD

Place the hare in a bowl and season it generously with pepper, salt and the blade of mace. Put it into a tall, thin casserole or an ovenproof jug. Add the bundle of herbs and the red wine or cranberry juice. Add the onions and enough water to come to just below the surface of the hare. Cover the jug or casserole closely, put it in a baking dish or ovenproof bowl with two inches of boiling water and place the whole into a preheated medium Gas Mark 3, 170 °C, 325 °F oven for 1½ to 2 hours until the hare is tender. Take out the pieces of hare, keep warm in a serving dish and pour the liquid through a sieve into a saucepan. Add the pinch of cloves, mace and cayenne, the redcurrant jelly and mustard, and the cornflour. Stir together over a gentle heat, bring to the boil and allow to thicken.

Pickled Mushrooms

WOODGATE FAMILY, CHIDDINGSTONE, 1765

Preserves were a crucial part of everyday cooking right up until the middle of this century, after which widespread refrigeration and air transport meant a constant supply of fresh out of season fruits and vegetables were regularly available. Indeed, many of the early recipe collections, books and lists are dominated by receipts for preserves and herbal mixtures intended to be used throughout the winter months when the raw materials were simply not available. This is an extremely simple recipe for pickled mushrooms which seems to work amazingly well. The instructions for rubbing them with a piece of flannel and salt derives really from the time when all mushrooms were picked in the wild. Indeed the mushrooms used for this may well have been Boletus or what the French call Ceps and the Italian Porcini. While they're available in European markets at the appropriate times, they're only available in this country to people willing to go out in the woods and find them, so I've adapted the recipe for our modern button mushrooms. Those don't need cleaning in quite the same way, otherwise the recipe follows pretty well the original version. It's worth making in significant quantities as they keep for a long time. You will need Kilner jars or other preserving jars with good rubber seals.

INGREDIENTS

3 lbs button mushrooms, unopened

2 tablespoons salt

2 blades of mace

8 peppercorns

1¹/₂ pints cider or white wine vinegar

METHOD

Trim the mushroom stems if necessary, place them all in a large colander and put over them all but a teaspoonful of the salt. Turn them over by hand, then pour over them a kettle of boiling water, shaking the colander, making sure all the salt is washed off. Allow to drain thoroughly and place them in a large thick saucepan. Add the teaspoon of salt, the mace and the peppercorns. Put them over a gentle heat, turning them regularly. As the mushrooms begin to give off some liquid, turn the heat up gently until the liquid is boiling off. Continue doing this for about 10 minutes until the mushrooms are dry. Pour the vinegar into the pan, making sure there's enough to cover the mushrooms, bring it to the boil and place the mixture into sterilised glass storage jars, making sure that there's enough vinegar to cover the mushrooms in each one. Close the lids, allow to cool. These keep for up to 2 years.

TO PICKLE MUSHROOMS TO PRESERVE THE FLAVOR

*The buttons must be rubbed with a piece of flannel & Salt, throw a little salt over & put them in a Stewpan with some Mace, & Pepper, as the liquor comes out shake them well and keep them over a gentle fire till all of the liquor be dried into them again, then put as much Vinegar into the Pan as will cover them, give it one warm & turn them into a Glass, or stone Jar, they will keep two years & are **delicious.***

Freggesse of Beanes & To Stew Celery

MARSHAM FAMILY, WHORNES PLACE, 17TH - 18TH CENTURY
UNKNOWN, 1818

These two vegetable recipes, although they come nearly 150 years apart, as the spelling alone indicates, are very similar except for the way that the sauce is thickened. In the early recipe an egg and butter emulsion, rather like a primitive hollandaise sauce, does the job for the beans, and in the 19th century recipe cream and a beurre manié provide the emulsion for the celery. Both recipes are very simple and provide substantial vegetable dishes, quite worthy of eating on their own as a first course or a light lunch, or vegetarian supper.

The beans concerned may well have been fresh haricot type beans but it is best made these days, I think, with runners cut into 1/2 inch chunks.

The six heads of celery mentioned in the recipe would have been less of a size than the celery we're used to now, so 2 modern heads of celery would feed 4 - 6 people quite well .

Bean Recipe

INGREDIENTS

1½ lbs runner beans, strung and cut into 1/2 inch slices

1/2 pint hot chicken stock

1 tablespoon butter

1 anchovy fillet

2 egg yolks

Salt and Pepper

METHOD

Place the beans in the hot chicken stock, bring to the boil and simmer for about 7 or 8 minutes until cooked but still crisp. Mash the anchovy fillet and butter together. Take a cupful of the liquid, mix with the anchovy and butter mixture and the egg yolks. Stir this together. Strain the beans into a colander and put the sauce mixture back into the saucepan. The heat already in it may be enough or it may need a little more heat to allow the sauce to thicken, but do not, under any circumstances, allow it to boil. Pour over the beans, season and serve.

TO FREGGESSE OF BEANES

Take 2 quarts of beanes boyle them and blanch them then putt them in a stew pan with some whitewine and gravey as much as will Cover them. Lett them stew till they are tender, Then take some of the Liquor that they are stewed in a piece of butter and the yolkes of 2 eggs and halfe an anchovis, put them in a dish and power this sawce upon them And soe send them up

TO STEW CELERY

Wash six heads and strip off their outer leaves either halve or leave them whole, according to their size; and into lengths of four inches. Put them into a stewpan with a cup of broth or weak white gravy; stew till tender; then add two spoonsful of cream, and a little flour and butter seasoned with pepper, salt nutmeg and simmer all together. Celery is a great improvement to all soups and gravies.

Celery Recipe

INGREDIENTS

2 good heads of celery, washed and trimmed

1/2 pint chicken stock

2 tablespoons cream

1 tablespoon each flour and butter, mixed together

Salt and Pepper

1/4 teaspooon grated nutmeg

1 tablespoon parsley, chopped

METHOD

Cut the celery heads into 4 inch lengths, splitting the butt end into four. Place them in a saucepan, pour the chicken stock over and simmer for about 10 to 15 minutes until still crisp but cooked through. Take the celery out of the pan and put into a serving dish. Add the flour and butter with the cream to the sauce, season with the pepper, salt and nutmeg, and stir until the sauce is shiny and smooth. Pour it over the celery and serve sprinkled with the parsley.

Trifle

GAMBIER FAMILY, LANGLEY, 1808, DELELAH TYLER, 1840

A trifle, the dictionary tells us, is 'a thing of slight importance' and that's certainly how one of the great British puddings got its name. A dish hardly worth considering, something you could throw together, not a serious piece of cooking. Well, from the number of recipes for trifle to be found in the early manuscript collections, people in the 18th and 19th centuries certainly were "considering" it quite a lot. And from the recipes themselves there was no lack of substance to the dish though, until very late in the 19th century it is, to the modern palate, a very monotonous confection containing virtually no fruit or other ingredients to give it zest or sharpness.

The one central requirement appears to have been stale cake or biscuits soaked in sherry, but it is possible to devise a conglomerate recipe, an amalgamation of different ideas which produces a rich but not cloying pudding to our modern tastes. The recipes quoted here range over a century, from the beginning of the 18th to the middle of the 19th century,and one of the regulars in most of them seems to be a 'boyld custard'. It's a good recipe to have anyway as real custard, made before Mr. Bird,whose wife was allergic to eggs, introduced his yellow cornflower confection, is a treat in itself. To be eaten with pies or puddings, or perhaps just on its own with a little sugar coating in the burnt cream style.

This is a very rich pudding and will feed at least 6 to 8 people.

AN EXCELLENT TRIFLE- GAMBIER FAMILY, LANGLEY, 1808
Take equal parts of wine & brandy, about a wineglass of each, or two thirds of good Sherry or Madiera, and one of spirit, and soak in the mixture four sponge buscuits & half a pound of macaroons and ratafias: cover the bottom of the trifle dish with part of these, & pour upon them a full pint of rich boiled custard made with three quarters of a pint, or rather more, of milke & cream taken in equal portions, & 6 eggs: lay the remainder of the soaked cakes upon it, & pile over the whole, to the depth of 2 or 3 inches, then sweeten & flavour slightly with wine only less than half a pint of thin cream (or of cream & milk mixed) wash & wipe the whisk, & whip it to the lightest possible froth: take it off with a skimmer & heap it gently over the trifle. Macaroons & ratafias ½ lb: wine & brandy mixed ¼ pint:rich boiled custard 1 pint: whipped syllabub light froth to cover the whole, short pint of cream & milk mixed: sugar dessertspoonfull: wine ½ glassfull.

INGREDIENTS

1/2 lb cooking apples, peeled and cored

1/2 lb dry sponge cake/fingers or almond ratafia biscuits broken up

1 tablespoon each brandy and madeira or 2 tablespoons sherry or orange juice or orange and cranberry juice substituted for a non-alcoholic version

3 tablespoons raspberry jam

1 tablespoon redcurrant jelly

1/4 pint double cream

Juice of half a lemon or lime

1 tablespoon of sugar, optional

4 tablespoons of water

a few baby almond biscuits or glacé cherries

FOR THE CUSTARD:

1 pint of milk

3 eggs

6 ozs sugar

1 teaspoon vanilla essence

1 tablespoon cornflour, mixed with a tablespoon of water

METHOD

Cook the apples in a nonstick pan with the water and no more than a tablespoon of sugar for those with a very sweet tooth. Cook until a lumpy purée and cool. Place it in the bottom of a large, preferably glass sided, bowl and crumble the cake fingers or biscuits on top. Mix the madeira and brandy or sherry or fruit juice and pour it over.

TO MAKE THE CUSTARD:

Whisk the milk, eggs, sugar and the vanilla together and heat gently. Add the cornflour to the mixture well before it boils and whisk. The custard will thicken and go glossy. It should be simmered for 2 or 3 minutes after coming to a gentle boil.

While the custard is cooling a little, spoon the raspberry jam on the cake and then cover with half the custard. Mix the recurrant jelly into the other half and pour that over to provide a different coloured layer. Whisk the cream and the lemon or lime juice together vigorously. It will froth up and form a whisked syllabub. With a large spoon, skim the froth off the top of the syllabub and pile it over the custard. Keep whisking and skimming until the whole of the trifle is covered. It can be decorated with some baby almond biscuits, because glace cherries, the modern decoration, seem to have been unheard of. Cool it for at least an hour. It can be chilled, but the syllabub tends to collapse after a while.

TO MAKE A TRIFLE - UNKNOWN, 1760S
Cover the bottom of your dish or bowl, with apples / buisquits cut in peaces Just wet them all through with Sack, then make a good boyld custard not to thick, and when could pour over it, then put a syllabub over that you may garnish it with ratafia cakes currantjelly and flowers

A TRIFLE - DELELAH TYLER, 1840
Lay your trifle dish with spunge cakes and macroons heaped up in the middle mix a table spoonful of Brandy to as much Madeira in a tumbler sufficient to moisten the cakes well (instead of Brandy you may put cherry or Raspberry Brandy to the Madeira) pour it over the cakes then take 3 large spoonsful of Raspberry Jam and little currant Jelly and 2 spoons ful of pounded sugar candy add to it by degrees a pint of cream or milk warm from the Goat, mix them well together and pour it over the cakes - By way of improvement you may pound finely a stick of cinnamon and add it to Jam also in case you have no bitter almonds in your macroons take 4 or 6 Peach Kernels blanched put them in a mortar and bruize them with a little of the cream or milk and mix this with the Jam, Lime Juice and Peel

Lemon Sponge

GAMBIER FAMILY, LANGLEY, 1843

Despite the name, this isn't a cake at all but really a lemon mousse. The dish is light and delicate and with modern techniques doesn't take the hour of whisking that's threatened here in the original recipe. It was originally intended for moulds, a kind of opaque jelly, but our taste for ornate centre-pieces has declined in the last century or so, so I think this is far nicest made and poured into pretty wine glasses or glass custard cups. It sets for serving as individual portions. It's particularly nice with light crisp, lemon flavoured biscuits.

INGREDIENTS

3/4 pint warm water

2 lemons, thin peeled or grated and juiced

1 oz agar agar or vegetable gelatine

1/2 lb sugar

2 egg whites

Small amount of candied lemon peel

METHOD

Place the gelatine or agar agar in 3/4 pint of water in a pan and stir - it should take about 5 to 10 minutes to dissolve. After the gelatine has softened add the juice of the lemons, the peel and the sugar. Keep stirring until it is thoroughly dissolved. Bring it to the boil and strain it through a sieve into a chilled basin. Put it in the fridge and allow to cool. It will start to thicken and jellify. When that's really underway, beat the whites of the eggs to a froth, not quite meringue thick but very substantial. Add the beaten eggs to the gelatine mixture and, using an electric whisk, whisk it for between 5 and 10 minutes in the chilled bowl. It will aerate and go like a pale lemon sponge. Before it completely sets pour it into the wine glasses or custard cups that it will be served in and decorate when cold with a little candied lemon peel.

LEMON SPONGE

Steep the peel of 2 Lemons in a pint of Water in which dissolve an oz of Isinglass & ½ lb of lump sugar - boil & strain it when cool add the juice of the lemons Beat the whites of 2 eggs to a froth & when the liquor is **cold** *& beginning to stiffen add the eggs & whisk it until it has the appearance of Sponge It sometimes takes an hour to beat but if allowed to be sufficiently cold before the Whites of Eggs are added it will seldom take more than 10 minutes - This quantity will sometimes make nearly 2 moulds*

Isinglass was a fish derived gelatine like substance, also used to preserve eggs

ROLLS BROTHERS'
PATENT ISINGLASS,

A CONCENTRATED PREPARATION FOR

Jellies, Blanc Mange, Soups, Preserves, &c.

DIRECTIONS FOR MAKING A QUART OF JELLY.

Soak in a pint and a half of cold water for a few hours one ounce of the Patent Isinglass, put the whole on a slow fire to dissolve; when just warm add loaf sugar to flavor, the rind of one lemon, pared thin, the juice of two strained, the white and shell of one egg, well beaten, and when beginning to simmer stir all together one way, and let them boil for a few minutes, strain through a jelly bag (previously wetted and squeezed dry) once or twice; adding, during the process, half a pint of wine.

TO MAKE SAME QUANTITY OF BLANC MANGE.

Soak one ounce as above, then lay it on a sieve, and when well drained add a quart of good milk, cinnamon, lemon peel, and loaf sugar to flavor, with a few drops of flavoring essence, set the whole on a gentle fire, stir one way or it will curdle, when scalding hot (but not boiling) pour the whole into a basin and let it settle for a time, and when partly cold strain it through a lawn or muslin sieve into moulds, leaving a cupful in the basin, that there may not appear any sediment when the moulds are reversed.

NOTE.—It will be requisite to use more Isinglass in summer, to meet the well known effect that a warm atmosphere has upon gelatizing substances.

It is necessary that the Isinglass be kept dry.

Queen's Cake Moulds, Hearts, Clubs, Crescents, Round, Diamonds, Oval, Square .... doz 0/9

DINNER-BELL AND FIREPLACE IN THE BANQUETING-HALL, OF PENSHURST, KENT.

Swiss Cream

GAMBIER FAMILY, LANGLEY, 1843

Swiss cream is one of a number of lemon flavoured mousse and cream type recipes to be found throughout the collections. Lemons have always been highly prized in Britain since the Romans first brought them, and in the Middle Ages fetched incredible prices - in 1290 a basket of 39 lemons went for £1, at a time when you could get 240 chickens for the same investment. By 1843, when this recipe was written, they were far more common but still highly valued. The recipe produces a very delicate cream dessert quite as refined as the reputation of the country for which it's named. As so many of these desserts, it's often nicest served in individual glasses as is suggested in the original recipe where the delicacy of the colour can be admired.

INGREDIENTS:

Juice and zest of 1 lemon

12 ozs double cream

3 ozs sugar

1 tablespoon cornflour

6 sponge fingers, broken up

2 tablespoons candied peel (preferably citron)

3 tablespoons orange juice (optional)

METHOD

Add the lemon zest to the cream and heat it gently. Add the sugar and allow that to dissolve. Let it simmer for 2 or 3 minutes to take on the flavour of the lemon zest. Mix the cornflour with the lemon juice, and whisk into the cream mixture thoroughly. Simmer for 3 minutes and allow to cool a little. Mix the sponge fingers with the candied peel reserving a few pieces for decoration. Place the sponge fingers and candied peel in the bottom of six wine glasses, (they can be moistened with a little orange juice), pour the cream on top and decorate with a couple of pieces of reserved citron peel. Chill for at least 2 hours before serving.

SWISS CREAM

Pare the rind of a lemon very thin boil it in 1/2 of a pint of cream with lump sugar to the taste - Let it stew a little time - Squeeze the juice of the lemon into a basen taking out the seeds - Mix into it very smoothly nearly a table spoonful of flour then pour the cream on it boiling hot, first taking out the lemon peel One person must stir the lemon juice & flour while another pours in the cream Keep stirring it for some time & let is stand to cool Serve it either in glasses with sweetmeats at the bottom or in a glass dish with sponge cake soaked in wine at the bottom & sweel meat on the Cake - The cream poured over all

Pare Plumb Cream

TWISDEN FAMILY, BRADBOURNE PARK, 1675-1750

No amount of research has so far revealed what a pare plumb was. The date of the recipe makes them earlier than almost any of the varieties of plums we grow these days, most of which were developments of the early 19th century. At the time this recipe was recorded by the Twisden family there were a variety of plums available, most of them, by our standards, small and sharp, rather like the damsons that had been in Britain since Crusaders brought them back in the Middle Ages. It's likely that pare plumbs were larger and pear shaped, making them easier to handle in this recipe. I think that greengages or the yellow cooking plums called Mirabelles would probably make the best equivalents today.

The sweet sharpness of the flavours and the richness of the texture are a wonderful combination.

INGREDIENTS

2 lbs golden or greengage plums, washed and cut in half

1/2 pint water

1 teaspoon rose water

6 eggs

6 ozs caster sugar

METHOD

Place the plums in the water and simmer them until they're tender and the stones float free. Scoop out the stones and remove any skins that have freed themselves as well. Purée the remaining mixture in a liquidiser or blender. Place in a very thick saucepan or double boiler with the rose water and sugar and stir until the sugar is thoroughly dissolved. Add the eggs gently, continuously stirring until the mixture thickens to the texture of double cream. Allow it to cool, it will set even thicker. Serve it in individual custard cups or ramekins.

PARE PLUMB CREAM
Take your pareplumbs & boyl th(e)m tender then pill of all the skins & take out all the stones & mash the pulp altogether, th(e)n put 3 spoon-full of Rose water and a pint of fare water and the yelks and whites of 6 Eggs well beaten then sweeten it with some fine sugger and sett it one the fire keeping it continually stirring one way till it thickens like cream then take it off and when cold dish it up -

Plum Bread

CHAMPNEYS FAMILY, LYMPNE, 1830S

Baking, especially bread, plays a surprisingly small part in the recipe collections. This is probably because it varied very little and was normally done by a specialist tradesman, even in a great house which would make its own bread on a regular basis. This was partly because bread ovens were not commonplace. They required a lot of fuel and quite a lot of space, and they were beyond the means of all but the comfortably well off - a smaller proportion of the population in those days than it is now. This recipe is especially interesting because it is an adaptation of part of a batch of already existing bread dough that would have been baked, probably twice a week. It is a special and possibly celebratory loaf. It's very similar in many ways to the traditional Celtic speckled breads or Bara Brith as they are known in Wales and where they are far more regularly eaten than in England. Although it's called plum bread it has no plums, but currants in it.

A Quattern loaf was the largest size of domestic bread, a 4 lb loaf about twice the size of what we would regard as a large loaf today. It's rather more in size than even an enthusiast would care to have for a currant bun so I have scaled the quantities down a little as well.

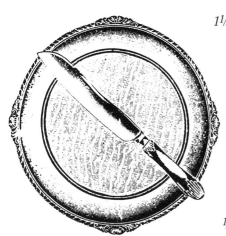

INGREDIENTS

1½ lbs strong bread flour

¾ pint warm water

1 teaspoon salt

1 oz fresh yeast or half a packet of dried yeast

1 egg, beaten

3 tablespoons milk

1 oz butter, softened

½ lb currants

3 ozs muscovado sugar

1 teaspoon caster sugar

METHOD

FOR THE BREAD DOUGH USING FRESH YEAST:

Mix the salt and flour together. Blend the yeast with a little sugar and a cupful of the warm water. When the yeast has frothed, add the rest of the water and the yeast mixture to the flour. Mix and knead until an elastic dough has formed. This should take about 2 minutes.

FOR BREAD DOUGH USING DRIED YEAST:

Mix the salt, flour and dried yeast. Add the warm water, mix and knead until an elastic dough is formed. Again this should take about 2 minutes.

FOR THE BREAD ITSELF:

Oil a bowl lightly and put either dough in the bowl. Leave aside to rise for an hour. When it's doubled in bulk, knead it again a little, add the egg and milk, and the butter. When that's incorporated, add the currants and sugar and mix well. The dough will be slightly sticky and may want a little more flour sprinkled over it to help make sure that the fruit is well mixed in. Place in a greased 2 lb loaf tin in a warm place, allow to rise for 45 minutes and bake in a pre-heated oven at Gas Mark 7, 210°C, 425°F for 45 to 50 minutes. Test for doneness by tipping out and knocking on the bottom. If it sounds hollow it's done, if not it needs another 5 to 10 minutes.

Mrs Laybornes Rich Rich Allmond Cake

TWISDEN FAMILY, BRADBOURNE PARK, 1675-1750

Mrs Laybornes cake, so simply but heartily endorsed by the repetition of its description, would have been a very special occasion cake indeed in the second half of the 17th century. Fine flour which is so clearly specified was hard to come by and would have been made by hand sifting the finest grind of flour to remove what would still, by our standards, be quite substantial chunks of wheat. Secondly, there was of course no baking powder available at the time - it wasn't available at a commercial level until about 1850, nearly 200 years later. Even the yeast that's used to raise this cake was still being taken from beer brewing as the sort of baking yeast that we're familiar with didn't become available for more than a hundred years as well. The yeast apart, the cake is close in many ways to the currant loaves and tea buns still much loved in Britain. It was a cake made on a pretty grand scale, the dry ingredients alone weighing 16½ lbs! On the smaller scale that I've suggested, I think that you'll find it a delicious and rich treat.

INGREDIENTS

1 lb plain flour, sieved

6 ozs ground almonds

6 ozs shredded candied peel (citron if possible)

12 ozs butter, softened

8 ozs double cream

1 oz yeast

4 tablespoons of warm water
and 1 teaspoon of sugar

1 teaspoon grated nutmeg

½ teaspoon each ground mace and cloves

4 ozs caster sugar

1 lb currants

6 egg yolks

4 egg whites

TO ICE IT:

4 ozs icing sugar

1 tablespoon orange flower water

2 ozs ordinary water

METHOD

Mix the ground almonds, the flour and the candied peel together. Rub into the flour and almond mixture 6 ozs butter until it's like coarse breadcrumbs. Melt the remaining butter in the cream, bring it to the boil and pour it all into the flour mixture. Mix the yeast with the warm water and teaspoon of sugar and leave to froth for 10 minutes in a warm place. Beat the 6 egg yolks and 4 whites until frothy. Sprinkle the spices over the flour mixture and then the caster sugar, then add the yeast mixture. Knead it thoroughly until it is a coherent dough, a little flour may need to be added to help the kneading process - a food mixer like a Kenwood does this job very well. When the dough is mixed, add the currants and mix through thoroughly. Leave it to rise in a warm place in an oiled bowl, well covered, for about 45 minutes until it about doubles in size. Knead it again briefly and put it into a greased or buttered 9 inch cake tin. Allow it to rise close to the top of the tin again and put it into a preheated oven Gas Mark 7, 210°C, 425°F. Turn the heat down immediately to Gas Mark 4, 180°C, 350°F and allow to cook for approximately 1 hour to 1 hour 20 minutes. Test it with a skewer to make sure that it's done - the skewer should come out clean. If not, leave it in the oven for a little longer. If it's browning too fast on the top, cover it with a piece of buttered foil or butter paper. Allow to cool for 5 minutes, turn onto a cake rack and allow to cool completely before eating.

FOR THE ICING:

Melt the sugar in the water, stir in the orange flower water and when the cake is cool, pour the icing over, spreading it with a wet palette knife.

MRS LAYBORNES RICH RICH ALLMOND CAKE

Dry 4 pound off Fine Flower in an oven and beatte itt fine and putt itt into a trey or bole and blanch a pound and halff off Allmonds (puting in now & then a little Sack to Keep them from oyling) and beatte them very Fine then rub them in the Flower and shreed a pound and halff off cittorne very Fine and strow itt in witth the allmonds or Flower and take a wine quartte off Creame and make itt redy to boyle then take itt off the Fire and stir in a pound and a half off Fresh butter and stir it till itt is all melted and you must rub into the Flower a pound and a halff off more butter then take 20 4(24) eggs and 18 off the whies and whip them very well with a pint of alle yeast that is thick and taken off the top and nott bitter and 3 pretty Large nuttmegs, 2 or 3 blades off mace, and a dussen Cloves all Finly beatten, and a pound of Fine sugger. Put in your butter and creame on one side, and the yeast and eggs on the other, and a Little above halff a pint off Sack must be beatte amongst the eggs and yeast, and when itt is well mingled and stir them all one way and when itt is well beatten up with wooden slise, then put in 4 pound and a halff off Currants washed and well dryed, then sett itt beffore a good Fire to rise halff anour and stir itt now and then to keep itt from Crusting, then stir itt well together beffore you put itt into the hoop, then sett itt into the oven to bake and Lett the oven be as hott as For Bread butt then take downe the heatte and one hour and a quarter will bake itt you must butter your hoop.

FOR ISEINGG

Take 2 partts suger and one off star whitte starch and Take eggs and oringe Flower watter and iff you please you may put a Little Musk or ambergre(s) inn your suger

Gateau de Pomme

The date's sufficiently late for the French name of the recipe and the listed donor (Mrs Danton) not to have any revolutionary connotations but as an apple cake the method itself is pretty radical. It's more what used to be known as a fruit cheese than a cake in the normal sense of the word. Despite the suggestion of setting it in a mould, I think you will find it easier to set in a dish you can bring to the table and serve from directly, rather than trying to turn it out as a jelly. You might try the rich custard sauce in the trifle recipe on page 91 to serve with it.

INGREDIENTS

16 eating apples (ours tend to be bigger than theirs were), peeled and cored

1¼ lbs sugar

1 glass of water

Rind of 1 lemon

METHOD

Cut the apples into quarter inch slices. Place the lemon, sugar and water in a big nonstick pan, bring to the boil and allow to start caramelising. Don't let it burn - it should be the colour of pale toffee. Put in the apples, stir them thoroughly, turn the heat right down and cover them, and leave it to cook for about 20 minutes. Stir again and go on cooking until the mixture starts to leave the sides of the pan. Pour it into an attractive serving dish, smooth the top and allow it to set for 4 hours at least before serving. It can be refrigerated to advantage.

GATEAU DE POMME
Mrs Danton

*Take 18 good sized apples, cut them quite thin,
likewise the rind of a lemon, then take 1lb and
a ¼ of lump sugar to a glass of water Set it on
to boil till it gets rather brown then put in the
Apples. Set it on to boil till it forms quite a jelly
Set it in a shape to cool and serve with a rich
custard round the dish*

Mr Pankhurst's Sider

MARSHAM FAMILY, WHORNES PLACE, 17TH-18TH CENTURY

This recipe, collected in the heart of Kent at the beginning of the 18th century was clearly intended to make good use of the plentiful apple supply. Although it doesn't say so, the apples used would almost certainly have been special varieties grown for their aromatic flavours and uneatable sharpness, producing a long lasting, well flavoured, dry cider. They had names like Sweet Coppin, White Sour, Ellis Bitter and Slack Ma Girdle! If you're going to make this recipe in modern times I think the only solution is to use cooking apples which have at least the necessary degree of sourness or sharpness to them. You certainly need unpasteurised juice because the method is designed entirely to allow natural yeasts on the fruit skins and from the air to do the fermentation work and pasteurising will reduce your chances most dramatically. The best system, I think, is to acquire apples, preferably unsprayed, mash them in a food processor or, if you have one, some kind of fruit press, and take it from there.

INGREDIENTS

20 lbs unsprayed cooking or unripe eating apples

1 or 2 gallon preserving jars (available from homebrewing and wine making suppliers)

Airlock system

METHOD

Extract the juice either by using a juice extractor or putting the fruit into a food processor and then into a jelly bag, allowing the juice to run out from the pulp. In this case, squeeze the pulp hard to make sure every drop possible is removed. Put the juice into a glass, wood or china bowl that will contain it all and leave it somewhere clean but unenclosed for 7 to 10 days, more in cold weather. Ladle it out carefully into a preserving jar that will contain it all leaving any debris behind in the original bowl. Seal it with an airlock system in the top. Allow it to go on fermenting for about a fortnight. It should then stop bubbling. If it doesn't, decant it again, get rid of the debris and replace it in a clean vessel until it ceases to bubble. Then seal the vessel completely and leave it for about 2 more weeks until it has cleared. It may need to be drawn off a couple of times as the debris comes out of it. Keep the container as full to the brim as possible to reduce the chances of it starting to re-ferment. When it is clear, bottle it, leaving all sediment behind. A piece of fine muslin in the funnel helps to ensure this. Cork it securely and leave it in a cool dry place for at least a month to six weeks before consumption.

MR PANKHURST TO MAKE SIDER

Put the juice into an open Vessell as a tubb Cooler or any such thing let it remaine a weak or ten dayes or more according as the weather is th(e)n draw it of into hoggsheads leaveing behind all the settlem(en)t you can conveniently so let it work a fortnight or a little more & if it does not th(e)n scace (ie cease) working draw it of againe but besure fill y(ou)r hoggshead brime full constantly Leaveing it a weak or 10 dayes more tell it hath done working th(e)n stope it close up as may be so let it stand a fortnight or 3 weeks & if it fine not drawe it of still & let it stand another fortnight or 3 weeks & so still continue drawing it of once a fortnight or 3 weeks but be sure keepe the vessell brime full & it will sartainly be fine but some times much sooner th(a)n at others according to the weather wh(e)n fine bottle it & besure it be fine before you doe botle it. I repeat th(i)s so offen becase on th(i)s cheifly depends the makeing of good Cyder at th(i)s being done I will ingage the Cyder shall be good R Gosling

Soda Water

GAMBIER FAMILY, LANGLEY, 1808

By the end of the 19th century the Army and Navy catalogue supplying the British at home and in far flung outposts of The Empire would offer more than 150 varieties of soda and mineral water, including some designed exclusively for bathing! At the beginning of the 19th century, however, if you wanted something fizzy you had to either live near the appropriate spa town or make it yourself, and this is the recipe for soda water named for the bicarbonate of soda that it includes. It's worth making in slightly larger quantities than the half a pint in the original recipe as the ingredients are available in any chemist and are, in fact, what we now use in a slightly different proportion as baking powder. The recommendation to use it to form a seltzer or a fizzy lemon drink is good advice. The raspberry vinegar also mentioned in the original recipe was made by steeping 1 lb of raspberries in white wine or cider vinegar for a day and sweetening it with 2 or 3 tablespoons of sugar. It was the origin of the bright red syrup we still occasionally see poured over children's ice cream cornets and was used until the middle of the 20th century as a delicious base for summer drinks, combining a sweetness and sharpness that was, and still is, most refreshing.

INGREDIENTS

*1 pint fresh, preferably fil-
tered, water*

*1 scant oz each cream of
tartar and bicarbonate of
soda*

METHOD

In a jug, which allows for some frothing up, pour in the
water before adding the cream of tartar. Stir until thoroughly
dissolved. Add the bicarbonate of soda and stir. It will
immediately fizz up. Pour it instantly into a screw top bottle
and seal hard to keep the fizz.

SODA WATER Mr Lindsay
*Tartaric Acid 16 gr(am)s. Carbonat of Soda 16 gr(am)s. Water ½ pint. The Tartaric Acid & Soda
should be in powders. Put in the Tartaric Acid into the water, & when perfectly dissolved put in the
Soda, & stir it & it will effervesce.*
It may be taken with wine, Lemon Syrup, Raspberry Vinegar &c &c

Winter, then as now, began with a feast, but until recent times ended with a voluntary famine, Lent. The period of abstinence began on Ash Wednesday and didn't end until Easter Sunday. Most of us have lost sight of the fasting or its purpose, but the preceding self indulgence we still celebrate with Shrove Tuesday and pancakes (Mardi Gras, or Fat Tuesday is the French name.) Christmas of course dominated the beginning of Winter with the festivities lasting until the 6th January and Twelfth Night. Then, following the Medieval and Renaissance pattern, the celebrations reached their secular height with feasting and present giving. All this conspicuous consumption was in a sense, very practical in a couple of ways. Firstly, it offered an excuse to use the more perishable foods in a flurry of defensible self indulgence and secondly, it really did give people a last big burst of fresh and vitamin rich food to last them though the leaner days to come.

Of course, the people who wrote, cooked and consumed the recipes in this book were, by the standards of their age very well-off, and in many cases extremely rich, so the levels of their self indulgences, as can be seen from some of the original recipes were really quite considerable. It's important to remember, though, in what were usually small communities these feasts were often shared with neighbours, servants and visitors in a way that would seem extraordinary to us in our nuclear familied age. So these recipes might at high days and holidays have been sampled by a wide and grateful assembly.

Observations on December, 1765.

Last Quarter the 5th Day, at 4 in the Afternoon.
New Moon the 12th Day, at 3 in the Afternoon.
First Quarter the 19th Day, at 7 in the Morn.
Full Moon the 27th Day, at 6 in the Morning.

D.	⊙ R.	⊙ S.	
1	8 2	3 58	Set all Sorts of Stones, Kernels, &c. Plant Vines, and Stocks for Grafting; trench Ground and dung it for Borders.
2	8 3	3 57	
3	8 4	3 56	
4	8 5	3 55	
5	8 5	3 55	
6	8 6	3 54	Towards the End of the Month, sow Radishes, Carrots, and Lettice on warm Borders.
7	8 7	3 53	
8	8 8	3 52	
9	8 9	3 51	
10	8 10	3 50	Sow Cresses, Mustard, and other Sallad Herbs on a moderate hot Bed, and cover them with Mats.
11	8 10	3 50	
12	8 11	3 49	
13	8 11	3 49	
14	8 11	3 49	
15	8 12	3 48	Plant all Sorts of Trees, that shed their Leaves.
16	8 12	3 48	
17	8 12	3 48	
18	8 12	3 48	The Winter Quarter begins the 21st of *December*, at Noon.
19	8 12	3 48	
20	8 13	3 47	
21	8 13	3 47	
22	8 13	3 47	Old *Par's* Maxims of Health. Keep your Feet warm by Exercise, your Head cool through Temperance, never eat till you are a hungry, or drink but when Nature requires it.
23	8 13	3 47	
24	8 12	3 48	
25	8 12	3 48	
26	8 12	3 48	
27	8 11	3 49	
28	8 11	3 49	
29	8 10	3 50	
30	8 10	3 50	
31	8 9	3 51	B TERMS,

Observations on January, 1765.

Full Moon the 7th Day, at 6 in the Morning.
Last Quarter the 14th Day, at 6 at Night,
New Moon the 21st Day, at 10 in the Morning.
First Quarter the 28th Day, at 10 at Night.

D	⊙ R	⊙ S	
1	8 9	3 51	
2	8 8	3 52	In this Month uncover the Roots of Trees, and cover with Dung the Roots of new-planted Trees, to prevent the Frost from injuring them. Cut all dead Branches off Fruit Trees. Plant Quicksets, and cleanse Trees from Moss. Sow Cresses, Mustard, Radish, Letuce and other small Herbs, in warm rich Soil.
3	8 8	3 52	
4	8 7	3 53	
5	8 6	3 54	
6	8 5	3 55	
7	8 5	3 55	
8	8 4	3 56	
9	8 3	3 57	
10	8 2	3 58	
11	8 1	3 59	
12	8 0	4 0	
13	7 59	4 1	
14	7 58	4 2	Sow Hotspur Pease, put fresh Earth to your Sage, Thyme, and other sweet Herbs. Transplant young Fruit Trees, prune Vines; trench and soil Ground for the Spring.
15	7 56	4 4	
16	7 55	4 5	
17	7 54	4 6	
18	7 53	4 7	
19	7 51	4 9	
20	7 50	4 10	
21	7 48	4 12	
22	7 47	4 13	
23	7 45	4 15	Let not Blood, and use no Physick, unless there be a Necessity: Eat often, and avoid too much Sleep.
24	7 44	4 16	
25	7 42	4 18	
26	7 40	4 20	
27	7 39	4 21	
28	7 37	4 23	
29	7 35	4 25	
30	7 34	4 26	
31	7 32	4 28	A 2

Observations on February, 1765.

Full Moon the 5th Day, at 11 at Night.
Last Quarter the 13th Day, at 3 in the Morning.
New Moon the 19th Day, at 11 at Night.
First Quarter the 27th Day, at 7 at Night.

D	⊙ R	⊙ S	
1	7 30	4 30	In this Month remove Grafts of former Years Grafting. Cut and lay Quick Sets. Vines may be planted the Beginning of this Month and Fruit that grows on Bushes. Set all Sorts of Kernels and stony Seeds.
2	7 29	4 31	
3	7 27	4 33	
4	7 26	4 34	
5	7 24	4 36	
6	7 22	4 38	
7	7 20	4 40	
8	7 18	4 42	
9	7 16	4 44	Sow on shady Borders the Seeds of Polyanthus. Sow Beans, Pease, Corn Sallad, Marigold, Anniseeds, Radishes, Parsnips, Carrots, Onions, Garlick, Beets and Dutch Brown Letuce. Set Oziers, Willows, and other Aquaticks. Rub Moss off Trees after Rain. Cut off Caterpillars from Quicks and Trees, and burn them.
10	7 14	4 46	
11	7 11	4 48	
12	7 11	4 49	
13	7 9	4 51	
14	7 7	4 53	
15	7 5	4 55	
16	7 3	4 57	
17	7 1	4 59	
18	6 59	5 1	
19	6 57	5 3	
20	6 55	5 5	
21	6 53	5 7	
22	6 52	5 8	Be sparing in Physick, and let not Blood without absolute Necessity, and be careful of catching Cold.
23	6 50	5 10	
24	6 48	5 12	
25	6 46	5 14	
26	6 44	5 16	
27	6 42	5 18	
28	6 40	5 20	
29	6 38	5 22	A 3

winter

Soupe à la Reine

CHAMPNEYS FAMILY, LYMPNE, 1830S

Which Queen this recipe is named after isn't quite clear. It's seven years too early for Victoria and, from its French title, may well come from an earlier 18th century European recipe. I think it is important that the broth contain the flavours of the vegetables which will not be present in the body of the soup themselves so you do need to *make* the stock and not use a cube. The soup's clear white colour is one of its attractions but perhaps it's nicest set off with a little decoration on serving - parsley is obvious, a couple of very finely stripped pieces of the green part of a leek or some pale celery leaf are good alternatives.

INGREDIENTS

1 chicken carcass, cleaned plus 1 breast, skinned and cut into four

1 leek, cleaned

1 carrot, peeled

1 bay leaf

1 sprig each thyme, celery and parsley

2 pints of water

3 ozs long grain rice, washed

1/2 pint cream

1 tablespoon parsley or celery leaf, chopped

Salt and White Pepper

METHOD

Put the chicken carcass and vegetables and herbs into a saucepan with the 2 pints of water. Bring to the boil and simmer for an hour. Strain, pressing well to extract all the flavour. Add the rice to the broth with the chicken breast. Bring to the boil and simmer, covered for 20 minutes until the rice is thoroughly soft and the chicken well cooked. Place the whole mixture into a liquidiser or food processor and purée until very smooth. The puréed mixture can be pushed through a sieve, if a very fine soup is desired. Season generously with salt and white pepper and stir in the cream. Keep it warm over a double boiler. Do not allow it to boil once the cream has been added! Serve it with a decoration of celery or parsley.

WHITE SOUP OR SOUP A LA REINE
To some good strong Broth add as much Rice as will make it tolerably thick, with the white Meat of a Chicken pounded so fine that it may be rubbed thro' a Strainer along with the Rice - Then add half a Pint of good Cream, after the Cream is added the whole is to be put into a Vessel of boiling Water & there kept till it is wanted to be sent up. It must not on any account to be boiled over the Fire after the Cream is added to the Soup
The Rice must be well washed & blanched before it is put to the Broth.

Cheese Pudding

UNKNOWN, 1818

The early part of the 19th century, when this recipe was written, was a time of poor harvests and considerable social unrest. This is a cottage yeoman's recipe, not one from a great house, and it exhibits the virtues of taking a small quantity of readily available ingredients and turning them into a main meal for a family. It's a tradition that's continued, as I clearly remember eating an almost identical dish only 15 years ago near Sevenoaks, not 40 miles from Goudhurst, where this recipe was originally collected.

In fact, it's a kind of simple soufflé, created long before the confections of haute cuisine became fashionable in the great restaurants of London and Paris. It will rise, although not as spectacularly as a soufflé and should be eaten hot with a green salad or green vegetable to follow.

INGREDIENTS

5 ozs soft white breadcrumbs

3 ozs cheddar or gruyère, grated

4 ozs butter, melted

¼ pint milk

2 eggs, separated

Pinch of salt and pepper

1 tablespoon fresh parsley or chives, chopped

METHOD

Pour the milk onto the breadcrumbs. Add the butter, grated cheese and the yolks. Season generously and add the parsley or chives. Beat the whites until firm. Fold in the beaten egg whites, pile onto a buttered soufflé or pie dish and bake for about 45 minutes in a preheated oven Gas Mark 5, 190 °C, 375 °F, until a skewer or sharp knife put into the middle comes out clean.

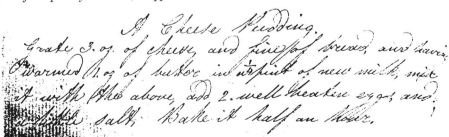

A CHEESE PUDDING
Grate 3oz of cheese, and five of bread, and having warmed 4oz of butter in a ¼ pint of new milk, mix it with the above, add 2 well beaten eggs, and a little salt, Bake it half an hour.

Kedgeree

HUSSEY FAMILY, SCOTNEY CASTLE, 18TH & 19TH CENTURY
KISHAREE, WHATMAN FAMILY, 1820

There is a certain amount of dispute about where Kisharee or Kedgeree came from. Clearly it was from the Indian subcontinent, equally clearly it was brought back by the servants of the empire. The general conclusion is that it was a dish made in different forms all over India, originally from rice and lentils. It still exists as a staple meal in areas as diverse as Bengal and Nepal but the addition of fish to it seems to have been an Anglo-Indian convention. By the late Victorian times Kedgeree could form an ornate centre-piece to a breakfast buffet but these two versions, about 40 years apart, date from the period when it would first have arrived in Britain and where, noticeably, the fish involved is not smoked. I think our tastes run, in this kind of mixed dish, to the added flavour bonus of smoking but then it was clearly, as the Whatman family recipe indicates, a way of using up leftovers. If you're into brunch or high tea, this is a perfect recipe, combining good flavours and a degree of lightness.

INGREDIENTS

¼ pint both milk and water

8 ozs long grain rice

4 hard boiled eggs, shelled

*12 ozs haddock
(smoked for preference),
boned and skinned*

2 ozs butter

1 teaspoon salt

*½ teaspoon cayenne
pepper*

½ teaspoon black pepper

1 tablespoon parsley

METHOD

Poach the haddock in the mixture of milk and water for a few minutes. When it's cooked, drain it, reserving the liquid. Measure the rice into a cup, place it in the pan and measure twice the volume in the same cup of the milk and water mixture from the haddock, topping up with more water if necessary. Bring the rice to the boil, don't add salt, and let it cook over a low heat until all the liquid is absorbed, about 12 to 15 minutes. Cut 2 of the eggs into quarters and chop up the other two. Flake the poached haddock and mix with the chopped eggs. Put the butter into a large frying pan, add the eggs, haddock and the rice and turn till mixed thoroughly but not too mashed. Season with the salt and peppers, pile onto a plate and decorate with the hard boiled egg quarters and a good tablespoon of parsley.

SCOTNEY CASTLE

The medieval remains of Scotney Castle, on an island in the river Bewl, have been a ruin since before the Hussey family have lived there. At first, in the 17th and 18th centuries they lived not in the castle, but in a house actually inside the old walls. The recipes were all collected at this time. In the 1830s Mr Edward Hussey undertook a huge improvement programme, building the present house, landscaping the grounds, romanticising the ruins and laying out the fantastic planting that is today such a feature.

KEDGEREE

A Breakfast cup full of Whole rice, boiled & strained -

4 Eggs hard boiled -

Mince all together with a Mincing Knife & a large Haddock boiled - (or any other cold fish) put a piece of butter in the Stew pan, & make the mince very hot Season it with salt & Cayenne pepper

KISHAREE

Fish Dressed a 2d time

Take a bit of any white fish that has been boiled, 3 tablespoonsfull of boiled rice & 2 hard boiled eggs chopped fine Add Pepper & salt & 2 ounces of butter. put all together & serve it up hot Any white sauce added improves this much

WHORNES PLACE AND THE MOTE, MAIDSTONE (HOMES OF THE WHATMAN FAMILY)

Whornes Place was a house built by the medieval Lord Mayor of London of the same name. Little remains of it now except the chancel of St. Michael's Church, which was originally the Tudor mansion's private place of worship. The Mote House in Maidstone is now a Cheshire Home, but its elegant park is part of the heritage of the people of Maidstone. Backing onto it is an 18th century industrial estate known as Turkey Mill, where James Whatman founded in 1739 the paper mill that produced the world famous 'turkey' paper.

To Rost a Rump of Beefe

MARSHAM FAMILY, WHORNES PLACE, 17TH-18TH CENTURY

'Cousen Dering' would have been Mary Dering or her mother who lived at Pluckley in East Kent on the high ridge overlooking the Built Plain. Clearly good cattle country and the enthusiasm for roasting a rump from one of them is clear from this detailed and delicious recipe. In terms of quantities, I think it's safe to say that a rump "cut large" would, to our eyes and purses, be beyond contemplation except when catering for a party of 40 or more. On a smaller scale it's still an excellent and interesting tasting recipe to those of us used to simply making gravy from the juices of roast meat. I think that roast potatoes and a green vegetable would probably be better than sliced lemon or cucumbers.

INGREDIENTS

4 lb rump or rib roast

1 teaspoon salt

6 ozs fresh breadcrumbs

2 ozs suet

1 teaspoon each thyme and parsley, chopped

1/2 teaspoon each cloves, ground pepper and ground mace

1 egg

FOR THE SAUCE:

1/2 pint beef stock

2 hard boiled egg yolks, mashed finely

2 ozs parsley, chopped

Grated rind and juice of half a lemon

Pinch of nutmeg, sugar and pepper

Half a finely, chopped small onion

2 ozs butter

1 oz flour, mixed with a little water

METHOD

TO ROAST THE BEEF:

Rub the joint with the salt and leave to stand for about 6 hours to mature. Mix the breadcrumbs, suet, thyme, parsley, cloves, pepper, mace and the egg together to make a forcemeat or stuffing. Roll it into balls, the size of a small marble, make some slits in the fat of the beef and insert the ball. Better still, make the forcemeat balls about twice the size of a marble, and put them under the beef to allow them to cook in the juices that run out; it improves both carving and temper. Roast in a preheated oven at Gas Mark 6, 200 °C, 400 °F for 15 minutes to the lb and 15 minutes over. If the forcemeat balls aren't stuffed into the meat, they may want to be turned as the cooking continues. Take it out and allow it to stand in a warm place, covered in a piece of foil for at least 20 minutes while the sauce is being made.

TO MAKE THE SAUCE:

De-glaze the pan with the beef stock. Mix the yolks with the parsley, lemon rind and lemon juice, nutmeg, sugar, pepper, finely, chopped onion and the butter. Place it in the pan and bring to the boil. Stir the flour mixture in and bring back to the boil and simmer till it thickens. Carve the beef in the normal way and serve with the sauce.

TO ROST A RUMP OF BEEFE *Cosen Dering*

Take a Rump of the fattest & best beefe you can let it be cut large Sprinkle it with salt a day or to th[e]n take a stale french lofe & grate it a q[uarte]r of a lb of of beefe suitt shreed small a little time & parsly shreed small a little Cloves Mace & peper beaten fine mix all thees together th[e]n w[i]th 2 egges make it up into balls & stuff the outside of the beefe deepe w[he]n tis roasted enough make y[ou]r sause w[i]th a pint of strong broath or gravey the yelks of 2 egges minced small a good handfull of parsly boyled & Choped a lemmon cut rind & all a hole nutmegg gratted a little peper beaten 3 or 4 shallots minced very small a little salt & a quarter of a pound of butter put all thees into the saucepan together & as heats shake in a little flower to thicken it th[e]n put the beefe into a dish & powre the sauce all over it th[e]n garnish it w[i]th sliced lemmon Barberys or cowcombers & send it up very hott

To Stew a Rump of Beefe

MARSHAM FAMILY, WHORNES PLACE, 17TH-18TH CENTURY

Mr Pankhurst, the cider enthusiast of page 102, offered the Marsham family a stewing recipe for a rump of beef. It seems an earlier recipe than Mary Dering's and I fear not one so adaptable to modern tastes, though it's included in its original form to show how varied the approach to a basic ingredient could be.

TO STEW A RUMP OF BEEFE *Mr Pankhurst*

First bone him th[e]n put him into a pan w[i]th 3 pints of water 12 anchovis 24 Shallotts w[i]th pepper & salt according to y[ou]r pallett w[i]th a bunch of sweet hearbs & a little lemon peele th[e]n cover it downe close in y[ou]r stew pan for 2 howers th[e]n take 2 pound of gravie beefe cut into slices & flower it very well & put it into a frying pan & frye it very browne flowering of it offen th[e]n take a bottle of Clarett & put it in a little at a time shakiing flower in it tell it is indefferent thick th[e]n take y[ou]r beefe out of y[ou]r stew pan & take the fat of very cleane th[e]n put y[ou]r gravie out of the frying pan Steaks & all into y[ou]r stew pan alltogether th[e]n slash y[ou]r beefe across like diamonds then keepe it stewing in y[ou]r pann 3 houres Longer then streyne of your gravie & take the fat off verie cleane then take juice of half a Lemon & 2 yelks of Eggs & butter & beat it together & mix it well w[i]th your sowce over a hott fire then serve it upp in y[ou]r dish w[i]th sliced Lemon

Stewed Pigeons

WHATMAN FAMILY, BOXLEY, 1820

Pigeons were one of the great standbys of great house cookery as well as of country cottage cuisine. The poor had to get pigeons as they could shoot or snare them, but the dovecots of the great houses, so much admired now, were in fact living larders. The doves or squabs were in fact our pigeons, often bred for exotic plumage but nevertheless kept for their eating as much as their decorative qualities. They were available all the year round and inside the hollow dovecots there were always ladders available for the cook or footman to climb up and help themselves to the snoozing poultry. They were an especially valuable source of fresh meat in the middle of winter, (before modern methods of refrigeration when nothing but salted meat was much available after Christmas. Pigeons are widely available in supermarkets these days without having to resort to shooting or dovecots and are the cheapest feathered game we can buy. This recipe stuffs them with forcemeat, effectively a stuffing enriched with suet but you can substitute vegetable fat if you prefer. The strongly flavoured sauce complements the rich darkness of the pigeon very well.

Serve a pigeon each on a piece of toast or fried bread if you choose, pouring the sauce over. Red Cabbage and mashed potatoes are ideal with this.

INGREDIENTS

4 pigeons, plus rinsed livers and hearts

6 ozs breadcrumbs

2 ozs suet

Pinch each thyme, parsley, salt and pepper and nutmeg

1 egg

FOR THE SAUCE:

2 cups chicken stock

1 anchovy fillet

1 onion, peeled and finely chopped

Pinch each cloves, mace and black pepper

1 oz each butter and flour, mashed together

METHOD

Mix the breadcrumbs, suet, thyme, parsley, seasoning and nutmeg together and bind with the egg. Chop the pigeons' livers and hearts and mix them with the forcemeat. Stuff the pigeons lightly. Heat a pan into which they will all fit together and oil it with a teaspoon of oil. Brown the pigeons, breast down, for 5 minutes, turning halfway. Put in the anchovy fillet, onion and the additional spices and stir together. Simmer for another 15 to 20 minutes until the pigeons are thoroughly done and tender to a knife at the breast and thigh. Remove the pigeons. Stir the butter and flour into the sauce and bring it gently to the boil. It should go shiny and glazed. Pour some sauce over each pigeon to serve.

TO STEW PIGEONS

Truss them for stewing, & fill them with forced meat not too full, put them in a sauce pan, or tossing pan with their breast downwards, cover them with small mutton broth, & let them stew gently, put in, an anchovey, two small Onyons, or one large, two or three cloves, a little whole black pepper & a blade of mace, let them stew altogether when done enough thicken your sauce with a little butter & flour, lay your pigeons in the dish & strain the sauce over them - The forced meat is made of Chopp'd suet, bread crumbled, & a little time & parsley, pepper & salt, & a very little nutmeg grated wetted together w[i]th Egg, Yolk & White, role them, & boil, or fry them as you like -

Boil'd Turkey

WHATMAN FAMILY, BOXLEY, 1820

Turkey, since its arrival in Britain at the beginning of the 17th century, has always been a popular fowl. It was often roasted and used at Christmas and other celebrations to replace or add to the more traditional goose. It had the advantage of a far greater ratio of meat to bone and the capacity to be cooked in other ways as well. Throughout the 19th century, boiled turkey with a variety of sauces was extremely popular and held to be very digestible. Modern research suggests this may be because of its extremely low fat content, the lowest of any normal domesticated meat. The original sauce recipe given here goes a long way to redress that however, containing beef marrow, cream and butter. For the modern version I'm going to suggest a rather lighter sauce, flavoured with celery, the ingredient that the late lamented Jane Grigson suggested, provided a sauce for turkey that was "mild but without insipidity".

Freshly cooked carrots, baby leeks and boiled potatoes are delicious with this.

PART 1ST TURKEY
INVITED OUT TO DINE.

INGREDIENTS

1 x 12 lb turkey

2 leeks, cleaned and trimmed

2 carrots, cleaned and trimmed

1 onion, peeled and stuck with 3 cloves

Washed trimmings from a head of celery

*4 parsley stalks ,
2 bay leaves,
6 peppercorns, 1 teaspoon salt*

FOR THE STUFFING

4 ozs breadcrumbs

2 ozs butter

4 ozs roasted chestnuts, peeled and chopped

6 oysters, shelled , optional

1 egg

1/2 teaspoon each salt and ground black pepper

1/4 teaspoon grated nutmeg

FOR THE SAUCE

2 ozs cream

1 oz each butter and flour

1 teaspoon lemon juice

4 sticks of celery, thinly sliced

1/2 pint of the turkey stock, strained

Salt and pepper

METHOD

FOR THE STUFFING:
Mix the breadcrumbs, butter, chestnuts, oysters (if being used), seasoning and the egg together to make a fairly coherent stuffing. Put this into the neck or crop end of the turkey and skewer securely closed.

FOR THE TURKEY:
Into a pan large enough to take the whole bird covered in water (a preserving pan is often useful for this), place the turkey, the vegetables and herbs. Fill carefully with water - if it will not cover the turkey, bring it at least to within an inch of the top. Cover the pan with foil or a lid, bring to the boil and simmer gently for 15 minutes per lb. A slow oven, Gas Mark 3, 170 °C, 325 °F, is fine for doing this if preferred to the top of the stove. When the turkey is completely cooked, (test for clear juices by pushing a skewer into the thigh), remove it from the liquid carefully and allow it to drain on a warm plate for at least 15 minutes before carving.

FOR THE SAUCE:
Fry the celery sticks gently in the butter for 5 minutes. Stir in the the flour and the lemon juice and season. Add the turkey stock and double cream. Stir and simmer for 2 or 3 minutes until the sauce has thickened. Then process in a food mixer or liquidiser. The celery can be left a little coarsely chopped if preferred.
Carve the turkey in the conventional way and serve with a little sauce on each plate and the remainder separately in a jug.

TO DRESS A BOIL'D TURKEY
When a Turkey is Truss'd stuff it with crumb of bread, marrow & roasted Chestnuts & Oisters, a little Nutmeg & Salt, an egg or two mix it up with butter & fill the breast of your Turkey & boil it - for the same stew some Oysters, & some veal gravey, some marrow first boil'd in a cloth, then thrown into cold water & cut into dice, a little cream, some butter & flower mix'd together to thicken it - when ready to serve up squeeze in a very little juice of Lemmon but dont put it over the fire after the Lemmon is in or it will curdle, pick out some of your largest Oisters Beard & set them w[i]th a small onyon stuck w[i]th Cloves 3 or 4 pepper corns, then dip them in the Yolk of an egg, role them in grated bread, fry them in Clarified butter & lay them in your dish

Yorkshire Christmas Pie

DELELAH TYLER, 1840

Christmas pies are legendary in Britain - little Jack Horner, you will remember, sat in the corner eating his - and throughout the second half of the 18th and the first half of the 19th centuries they were one of the great traditions for those who could afford them. The reason the name Yorkshire is almost always attached is because Yorkshire was a rich agricultural county full of produce but not many people, whereas London was the reverse. So at Christmas time a method had to be devised to move this produce from where it was grown to where it was to be consumed - not so easy a task in the days before refrigeration or sophisticated roads, let alone railways. This pie was the answer. Although it was encased in pastry, the pastry itself wasn't meant to be eaten but was an airtight seal, inside which the food was both cooked and transported, a large scale, early form of canning. The pie was opened at Christmas time and provided a delicious source of potted and cold meats for days to come. Some of them would have been eaten heated up, and some of them taken out and sliced down cold. The pie would not have been eaten at one sitting unless there were a huge number of people to feed as the quantities in the original provide over 30 lbs of meat without the other ingredients. It is however a delicious tradition and one that on a slightly smaller scale is worth practising even in the days of refrigeration and air transport. I've given a version of the original at full size if you fancy a little bit of culinary archaeology and a smaller lighter version that would generously feed a buffet party of 20. In this case, you're meant to eat the pastry as well. I ought to note that while I'm not accusing Mrs Delelah Tyler, who collected this recipe in 1835, of plagiarism, it does in places bear a remarkable resemblance to the recipe for a pie of the same name published in Hannah Glasse's *The Art of Cookery Made Plain*, at the end of the 18th century.

It should be noted that the bones from all the ingredients will make the most incredible and vast quantity of stock.

Original Version

INGREDIENTS

1 x 14 lb turkey

1 x 8 lb goose

1 x 6 lb roasting chicken

1 x 3 lb pheasant

1 pigeon

1 hare, jointed with the breast bones removed

4 mallard or other wild duck

all boned by slitting the skin along the back and cutting the flesh off the carcass and leg and wing bones progressively, a good butcher given enough notice might even be willing to make the attempt

6 lbs plain flour, 2 tablespoons salt, mixed together

1 dessertspoon each powdered mace, nutmeg and ground black pepper

1 teaspoon ground cloves

4 lbs butter, cut into pieces

2¼ lbs white fat (vegetable shortening rather than lard)

Generous quart of water

1 dessertspoon salt

1 egg, beaten

Salt and pepper

METHOD

Season the meat generously with the salt and spices, and layer up with the turkey, skin outermost, on the outside, then the goose, chicken, pheasant and pigeon at the end. Wrap the turkey around as best as possible. Take the breast and legs off the mallard and discard the carcass. Place the white fat in the water and bring it to the boil. Put the flour and salt into a large basin and pour the fat and water mixture when it comes to the boil over the flour in one go. Mix it rapidly together with a wooden spoon or electric blender. When it's cool enough to handle, but still warm, take a quarter of the pastry for the lid and use the remainder to line a large cake tin or casserole, into which the birds will go. This pastry must be worked while its still warm. Put in the turkey roll and surround it with the pieces of hare and duck, filling in the gaps as best as possible. Place the butter over the top of the mixture. Roll out the lid and seal carefully all round the edges, using the beaten egg to achieve this. Make a small hole in the centre to allow steam out and glaze the pie with the rest of the beaten egg. Put it into a preheated hot Gas Mark 6, 200 °C, 400 °F, oven and cook for 2 hours, turning the temperature down after that to Gas Mark 4, 180 °C, 350 °F and cook for the next 4 hours. Remove from the oven carefully and allow to cool for at least 24 hours. It can be refrigerated after that but will keep for a couple of weeks in a cool place without the benefit of the fridge.

A YORKSHIRE CHRISTMAS PIE

Take a fine large Turkey a Goose a large fowl a Partridge and a Pigeon and bone them all nicely - Beat ½ oz of Mace ½ oz Nutmeg ¼ oz Cloves ½ oz white pepper and 2 large spoonsful of salt all mixed together open all the Fowls down the back, lay the Turkey on the dresser season it in the inside lay the Gooses breast downwards in the Turkey then season the Goose, put in the Fowl in the same way, then the Partridge, then the Pigeon. Close them together to make them look like a whole Turkey as well as you can. Case and bone a hare and cut it in pieces with six woodcocks, moor Game or small wild fowl all boned. Make a bushel of flour with 10 lbs of butter into a paste as directed. Make the bottom and sides very thick and raise it as high as you can put it in some seasoning then lay in the Turkey &c breast uppermost - lay the Hare on one side and the Game on the other sprinkle seasoning over all put 4 lbs butter over the top - lay on a thick lid with whites of Eggs over all, put paper over it and bake it in a hot oven for 6 hours let it stand till cold before you cut it -

Yorkshire Christmas Pie

Modern Version

INGREDIENTS

1 turkey breast, boned

1 x 6 lb chicken

1 pheasant

1 lb piece of cooked ox tongue

1 duck

1 teaspoon salt

1 teaspoon each ground, mace, nutmeg and black pepper

1/2 teaspoon cloves

1^{1}/2 lbs butter, cut into small pieces

2 lbs sifted plain flour, 1 teaspoon salt, mixed together

12 ozs white fat (flora or similar)

3/4 pint of water

1 beaten egg

METHOD

Open out the turkey breast. Take the meat off the chicken, pheasant and duck, leaving the bones in the legs if so desired. Season the turkey, chicken and pheasant with the salt and spices. Using the tongue as a centre-piece, pack the pheasant and chicken meat around it and wrap as best as possible in the turkey breast. Melt the white fat in the water and pour it, when boiling, over the flour and salt. Stir with a wooden spoon or electric beater until smooth. Allow to cool until comfortable to handle and use three quarters of the pastry to line a large cake tin with a removable base, or a raised pie tin. Place the turkey roll into the pastry, add the pieces of duck round it and the 1^{1}/2 lb butter over the top. Roll out the remaining pastry and use some of the beaten egg to help make a careful seal all round the pie. Cut two slits in the top and decorate the pastry with the trimmings. Glaze with the rest of the beaten egg and cook in a preheated hot oven, Gas Mark 6, 200 °C, 400 °F for 30 minutes, turning the heat down to Gas Mark 4, 180 °C, 350 °F, and cook for a further 1^{1}/2 -2 hours. Allow to cool thoroughly for at least a day before serving.

To Bake a Goose

MARSHAM FAMILY, WHORNES PLACE, 17TH-18TH CENTURY

This recipe is clearly written by a cook, remembering what he or she had done, and forgetting to tell us to add the ginger seasoning until at the end of the recipe. That flavouring, and the whole style of the dish, suggests that it was from an early tradition. Geese were, in the 17th century, eaten roasted on high days and holidays by ordinary people and on numerous occasions by their richer compatriots. This recipe is more similar in many ways to the French confit d'Oeie, or preserved goose, which has been raised almost to an object of veneration in modern France as the epitome of country style cooking. In Britain a goose is a rare bird these days, although it certainly wasn't in the 17th and 18th centuries. In those days flocks of hundreds of thousands used to be walked down from the East Anglian counties where they were especially bred for the Michaelmas and Christmas markets in London. It's a fascinating sideline to know that they were shod for this by dipping their feet in warm tar to prevent their perambulations wearing out their natural webs.

If you like goose this is an attractive recipe, not least because in many people's minds it's best eaten cold, being a fatty and very rich bird. Some lightly spiced apple sauce and hot baked potatoes go wonderfully with it, and if you're into bean dishes and cassoulet, it works perfectly as the preserved goose addition to such continental luxuries. If eating it cold, scrape off the fat with a knife before serving.

INGREDIENTS

1 x 7 - 8 lb goose, jointed, keeping the breast in two pieces

8 bay leaves

1 lb butter, cut into chunks

1 tablespoon caster sugar

1 teaspoon powdered ginger

12 ozs onions, peeled and sliced

1 glass apple juice

10 ozs plain flour

5 ozs water

Salt and Pepper

METHOD

Rub the meat with some pepper and salt. Place half the bay leaves in the bottom of a large casserole with a well fitting lid. Add the onions and the goose, with the ginger and caster sugar sprinkled over it. Put on the remaining bay leaves, the butter, and a glass of apple juice or white wine. Mix the flour and water together into a paste and use that as a seal on the lid of the casserole, spreading it in a sort of sausage around the edge and pressing the lid well down. Bake it in a slow preheated oven, Gas Mark 3, 170°C, 325°F, oven for 3 to 4 hours and allow to cool before breaking open the covering. The goose should be almost submerged in the cold fat, which will preserve it for a fortnight in the fridge or, if it is completely submerged and the seal unbroken, for up to 2 to 3 months.

TO BAKE A GOOSE

Take a goose & bone him then take a new earthen pott & first lay in 3 or 4 bayes leaves then lay in the goose & break in a lb of butter an ounce of sugar tw[o] onions a good quantity of pepper salt so season it high, a pint of whitewine & upon it 13 or 14 bay leaves more soe past it up, & let it be very baked & soked when tis Cold tis an excellent dish. Put in some powdered ginger which was forgot

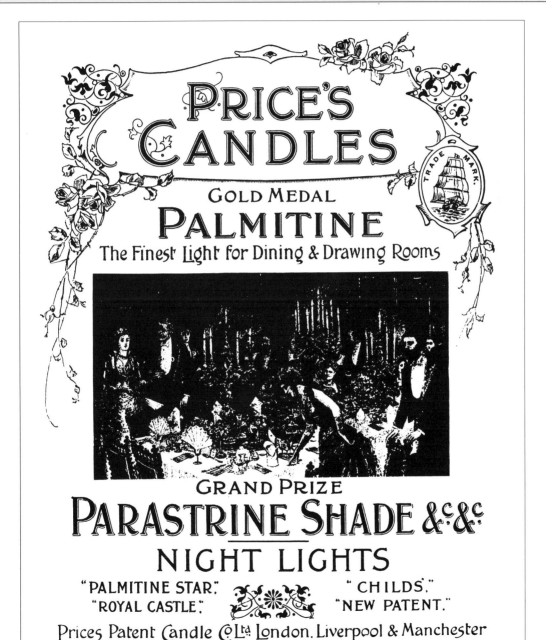

Pease Pudding

DELELAH TYLER, 1840

The tradition of cooking peas in Britain has two distinct and separate strands. The modern one, for green peas, the adjective often used to define the difference, came via France from Italy when Catherine de Medici brought them with her from Renaissance Florence. The older tradition is one for dried peas, peas eaten rather like we use haricot or butter beans today. They were a high protein, highly nutritious and very storable commodity, grown on a large scale from early Medieval times. That tradition continues today in Britain, certainly in the North, in the form of mushy peas in most fish and chip shops. Also there is pease pudding, still eaten regularly in the North and Scotland as one of the great accompaniments to boiled meats, especially in the winter time when it adds warmth and fibre to the diet.

I think this recipe is actually delicious enough to be eaten on its own as a kind of hot vegetable paté as a first course but it's also great with sausages or hot salt beef as the original suggests. Mrs Tyler asks, why not eat it with roasted pork? And I think the answer is that it would be too rich to eat with a greasy meat.

THE TYLER FAMILY, RELATED TO THE ROPERS

Delelah Tyler was the wife and widow of C.H. Tyler and, for the early 19th century, she was a lady of some determination, because she managed to obtain from the College of Arms a grant allowing her to add the Tyler arms to those of the Benwell family. The most important connection though is to the Ropers, who were the descendants of the daughter of Sir Thomas More, the Chancellor of England whom Henry VIII executed because he would not agree to comply with the king's desire to wed Anne Boleyn. Shortly after she obtained her Grant of Arms in 1840, or thereabouts, Mrs Tyler wrote her small recipe book. She was well read and her book shows that her recipes were influenced by other books of that period.

INGREDIENTS

1 lb dried split yellow or green peas, soaked for 4 hours

1 egg, beaten

1 oz butter

1 dessertspoon salt

1 teaspoon pepper

METHOD

Place the soaked peas in a non stick saucepan, cover them with cold water, at least 2 inches deep, bring them to the boil without seasoning and simmer them till they're tender. Modern dried peas will probably be ready in about 1½ to 2 hours. Drain them, leaving them moist and purée them in a food processor or through a mouli legumes. Add the egg and the butter, season generously with salt and pepper and mix thoroughly. Place them in a buttered, quart pudding basin, put a pleated piece of greaseproof paper over the top, put the basin into a saucepan with 3 inches of boiling water and boil for 1 hour. A long piece of folded foil under the basin enables the basin to be removed easily. Serve it with a spoon from the basin or turn it out to serve in slices. It can also be cooked in individual sized ramekins for about 30 to 40 minutes in the same manner.

PEASE PUDDING

Put a quart of split peas into a clean Cloth: do not tie them up too close, but leave a little room for them to swell: put them on to boil in Cold water, slowly till they are tender: if they are good peas, they will be boiled enough in about two hours and a half, rub them through a seive into a deep dish, adding to them an egg or two, an ounce of butter, and some pepper and salt; beat them well together for about ten minutes when these ingredients are well incorporated together; then flour the cloth well put the pudding in, and tie it up as tight as possible, and boil it an hour longer - It is as good with boiled Beef as it is with boiled Pork - and why not with roasted Pork?

Pancakes

HUSSEY FAMILY, SCOTNEY CASTLE, 18TH CENTURY
MARSHAM FAMILY, WHORNES PLACE, 17TH-18TH CENTURY

Winter contained, as well as Christmas, the feasting season that marked the beginning of Lent; that period of abstinence where meat was eschewed and luxuries like cream and eggs were often avoided. Before the beginning of Lent was Carnival and Shrove Tuesday, with the great tradition of pancake day when all the luxuries were to be used up in the pancakes. Here is an amalgam of two recipes for such pancakes from two original receipts about 100 years apart. In the originals, they are different in detailed quantities, but almost identical in general approach. The later version from the 18th century Hussey family were designed to be thinner and when stacked up looked like a packet of writing paper with the slightly crinkly edges that it would have had in the 18th century. The main point of difference is whether or not you should strew sugar on the pancakes! My own vote is for yes, and a quarter of a lemon per person to squeeze over them. If you build up a stack of pancakes like the 'quire' it was traditionally served cut into wedges like a cake, rather than the pancakes being individually rolled up and served. These pancakes are very rich compared to our habit - more like thin sweet omelettes than a flour based batter and so need little else to enhance them.

INGREDIENTS

4 ozs butter

16 fl ozs cream

3 ozs plain flour

4 tablespoons orange juice

1 tablespoon caster sugar

1/2 teaspoon grated nutmeg

8 egg yolks, 6 egg whites
(size 3)

METHOD

Melt the butter in 12 fl ozs of the cream and add the orange juice, caster sugar and nutmeg. Beat the egg yolks and the egg whites together and stir the flour into the remaining cream until it is smooth. Put the flour mixture in a large bowl, sieve the eggs onto that and stir in the cream mixture when it has cooled a little. Whisk it thoroughly and leave it to stand for 30 minutes in the fridge. Put a knob of butter in the pan, let it heat thoroughly and stop sizzling. Pour a scant ladleful of batter in, swirling the batter round the pan so that the pancake is as thin as possible. Leave it to set, turn it with a spatula, cook for another 30 seconds and put it onto a warm plate. Sprinkle a little sugar and repeat the process. The pan shouldn't need to be rebuttered once the pancakes are being produced.

Lemon Creams

TWISDEN FAMILY, BRADBOURNE PARK, 1675-1750
UNKNOWN, 1818,
WHATMAN FAMILY, BOXLEY, 1820

Throughout the winter, from the 16th century onwards, lemons were regarded as one of the great antidotes to the salted and preserved foods which so many people had to live on. They were thought to 'cleanse the blood' and were incorporated, when they could be found and afforded, into a wide variety of dishes. The collections are full, in particular, of recipes for lemon cream, many of them almost identical. I've chosen three of them.

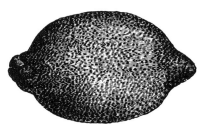

The most interesting comes from the Twisden family and it takes advantage of the fact that lemon juice will curdle cream. It produces therefore rather an unusual layered dish, rather like an early form of lemon yoghurt, with some almond slivers to add crunch.

The other two recipes are almost identical to each other in substance, although the wording is quite different. They produce a smoother, thicker cream because it is set by the egg yolks included. I have produced an amalgam of the two recipes.

INGREDIENTS

1 pint double cream

1 lemon

4 ozs slivered almonds

4 ozs caster sugar

METHOD FOR RECIPE 1

Bring the cream to the boil and allow it to cool. Add the juice of the lemon and allow it to separate. Drain it through a strainer. Toss the slivered almonds in a dry frying pan until they lightly colour. Mix the sugar into the lemon curds and put a layer of curds into a small glass bowl followed by a third of the almonds, another layer of curd, another third of the almonds, another layer of curd and finish with the almonds sprinkled over the top for decoration. Let it chill for at least an hour or two before serving.

INGREDIENTS

16 fl ozs double cream

2 egg yolks

4 ozs caster sugar

Grated rind and juice of 1 lemon

METHOD FOR AMALGAM

Heat the cream gently with the lemon rind and sugar until the sugar dissolves. Beat in the yolks of the eggs and bring to just below the boil. Allow to simmer for a couple of minutes and then cool. As the cream cools, stir in the lemon juice, being careful to continue stirring as it cools because otherwise it might separate. Pour into tall thin glasses and chill for 2 hours before serving.

TO MAKE LEMON CREAME

Boyle your creame and when itt is halff Cold turne itt with the Juce off a Lemon to a Curd then drane itt through a strainer then beatte some blanched almonds and so lay one Laying off Curd and a Laying off suger and another off almonds and another off suger and another off Curd and so do till the dish bee full and suger scraped over itt and sarve itt in.

LEMON CREAM

Take a pint of thick cream and put it to the yolks of two well beaten [eggs] four ounces of fine sugar and the thin rind of a lemon, boil it up then stir it till almost cold; put the juice of a lemon in a dish or bowl, and pour the cream upon it, stirring it till quite cold.

LEMMON CREAM Mrs Dalton

Take a pint of cream - the yolks of two eggs and a ¼ pound sugar - boil this with the rind of a Lemmon cut very thin in it - when almost cold take out the rind & put in the juice of the Lemmon by degrees and it will turn keep it stirring till it is quite cold and then put it into glasses

Chocolata Creme

MARSHAM FAMILY, WHORNES PLACE, 17TH-18TH CENTURY

At the time the Marsham family collected this recipe, chocolate was a great luxury and usually used as a drink in the Chocolate Houses of London and other cities.

INGREDIENTS

16 ozs double cream

4 tablespoons sugar

1 oz cocoa powder

2 ½ ozs grated bitter chocolate

1 tablespoon water

2 egg yolks

1 egg white

METHOD

Mix the sugar with the cream and bring it gently to the boil. Beat the egg yolks with the egg white until frothy. Stir the cocoa with a tablespoon of water until smoothly blended. Add it to the eggs and add a couple of tablespoons of the hot cream. Mix thoroughly together and pour back into the cream. Stir it for a moment and place in a food processor or liquidiser with the grated dark chocolate. Process until smooth, pour into custard cups or small chocolate cups and leave it to cool for at least 3 to 4 hours before eating. It will retain a slightly grainy texture.

Duke of Cumberland Pudding

UNKNOWN, 1818

Which Duke of Cumberland this pudding is named after is not clear and I can find no record of it in any of the expected places or sources. It seems likely that it may recall the tastes of the Butcher of Culloden who was such a force in Britain in the middle of the 18th century. Whatever the provenance, it's a light fruity pudding especially if made with modern suet or vegetarian suet rather than that drawn from sheep's kidneys as the original suggests. With our lighter tastes you don't need double the quantity to feed four hungry or six ordinary people well.

Cream or a light custard finish the pudding off excellently.

Duke of Cumberland Pudding.

Mix six ounces of grated bread, the same quantity of Currants, well cleaned and picked, the same of sheep suet, finely shred, the same of chopped apples, and a lb. of lump Sugar, six eggs, half a nutmeg, a pinch of salt, the rind of a lemon minced as fine as possible, and citron, orange, and lemon, a large spoonful of each cut thin, Mix thoroughly and put into a bason, cover very close with floured cloths, and boil three hours, serve with pudding sauce, and the juice half a lemon boiled together. N.m. double the above quantity just fills my large mould.

INGREDIENTS

6 ozs white breadcrumbs

6 ozs currants

6 ozs suet or vegetarian suet

6 ozs cored and chopped, but not peeled apples

6 ozs caster sugar

6 eggs

1 teaspoon grated nutmeg

Pinch of salt

Grated rind of 1 lemon

3 tablespoons mixed peel

METHOD

Mix the breadcrumbs, currants, suet, apples and the sugar together. Beat the eggs, stir in the nutmeg, the salt and lemon rind, and pour onto the breadcrumb mixture. Mix thoroughly and add the mixed peel. Butter a pudding basin and place the mixture in it. Cover with a folded, pleated piece of greaseproof paper, put into a saucepan with 3 inches of boiling water and cook for 2 to 2 1/2 hours before turning out and serving. In a pressure cooker this will take between 45 minutes to 1 hour.

DUKE OF CUMBERLAND PUDDING
Mix six ounces of grated bread, the same quantity of Currants well cleane'd and picked the same of sheep suet, finely shred, the same of chopped apples, and also of lump Sugar, six eggs, half a nutmeg, a pinch of salt, the rind of a lemon minced as fine as possible, and citron, orange and lemon, a large spoonful of each cut thin. Mix thoroughly and put into a bason, cover very close with floured cloths, and [b]oil three hours, serve with pudding sauce, and the juice of half a lemon boiled together.

Oxford Pudding

WOODGATE FAMILY, CHIDDINGSTONE, 1765

In this recipe, smaller quantities of similar materials for the Duke of Cumberland pudding were mixed, but without the apples and just 2 eggs. They were then made into large balls and fried in butter. For this recipe I suggest that you use 4 oz each of the ingredients on page 131 and after the balls have been fried in butter to a light brown, place them in the oven to bake for about 20 minutes before eating them. A bit heavy and doughy for modern tastes.

Cabinet Pudding

GAMBIER FAMILY, LANGLEY, 1808

The precise quantities in this recipe are not much use to us because of the introduction of Imperial Measures after Victoria became Queen Empress. This increased the volume of liquids in the pint and quart and gallon by 25% from 16 ozs to the pint (still the case in America) to 20 ozs. The pudding, also known in other collections as Charter or Chancellors Pudding, is best known for the cherries and angelica that were often used to enhance it.

It is delicious with jam sauce or a light custard.

INGREDIENTS

4 ozs large raisins (and glacé cherries and angelica pieces, optional)

6 ozs sponge cakes, broken into small pieces

6 ozs almond or ratafia biscuits, crumbled

1½ tablespoons candied peel

½ pint single cream

½ pint milk

2½ ozs caster sugar

4 egg yolks

3 egg whites

METHOD

Butter a quart pudding basin and place the raisins (and cherries and angelica) in equal quantities around the basin. Put the sponge cake, with the biscuits into a separate bowl. Bring the milk and cream to the boil, and add the caster sugar. Off the heat, beat in the 4 egg yolks and 3 egg whites and strain through a sieve onto the cake mixture. Stir till thoroughly soaked in and incorporated, add the candied peel and pour into the basin. Cover with a piece of pleated greaseproof paper and steam or boil for an hour in a saucepan with 3 inches of water or for 25 to 30 minutes in a pressure cooker. Allow to stand for a moment before turning out. The pudding is very delicate and can break at this point.

CABINET PUDDING

Split & stone 3 doz fine jar raisins, or dried cherries, and place them in a pattern in a thickly buttered quart mould, next slice and lay into it three penny sponge cakes, add to these 2 oz. of ratafias ¼ lb maccaroons 1½oz candid citron sliced thin, the yolks of 4 eggs, and the whites of three thoroughly whisked, mixed with ½ pint of new milk, then strained to ½ pint sweet cream, sweetened with 2½ oz pounded sugar, these ought to fill the mould exactly. Steam the pudding or boil it very gently one hour, let it stand a few minutes before it is dished that it may not break and serve with good wine or brandy sauce

Gingerbread

TWISDEN FAMILY, BRADBOURNE PARK, 1675-1750

Gingerbread became popular because of the Jamaican connection with Britain. The sugar, the treacle, the nutmegs and the ginger all came from that incredible spice island that created so much wealth that it was known as the Jewel of the British Empire, even when we owned most of India and North America. This, as so many early recipes, is made on rather a grand scale in its original form. Also, as they didn't have the benefit of self raising flour there was a fair chance that it would come out rather like a brick, as the author notes. The modern version, I hope you'll find, is lighter though generously spiced. 'Searching' the sugar and the flour, by the way, was to make sure that there were no extraneous objects like bugs in it, before you used it to cook with.

The grated rind and the juice of an orange is an optional extra, which I think improves the cake and should be mixed in with the treacle and eggs. It may sink a little in the middle when it comes out of the oven but when cool will taste delicious. It improves when left wrapped for 4 to 5 days.

INGREDIENTS

6 ozs caster sugar

1 generous teaspoon ground ginger

1/2 teaspoon each ground cinnamon and nutmeg

8 ozs self raising flour

7 ozs treacle

1/4lb butter, melted

2 eggs, beaten

Grated rind and juice of orange, optional

METHOD

Mix together the sugar, the spices and the flour. Pour in the butter with the treacle and the eggs. Mix thoroughly together and put into a buttered loaf tin and line with bakewell paper. Bake it in a preheated oven at Gas Mark 3, 170 °C, 325 °F for 1 1/2 hours or a little longer if the cake is preferred dry.

TO MAKE GINGER BREAD

Take 3 quarters of a pound of suger searched one ounce of beaten Ginger sifted half anounce of Cinamon two Nuttmegs mingle these w[i]t[h] about 2 quarts of fine flower that is well dryed then put in 3 pound of treacle 3 quarters of a pound of melted butter. six eggs mix all these together Lett it be stiff enough to make up into ro\a/ls yo[u]r oven must be pretty quick or else it will be heavey half an our will bake it it should be put upon double Cap paper buttered you may put in oringe or Cittorn if you please yo[u]r flower should be searched after it is dryed -

Mince Piees

TWISDEN FAMILY, BRADBOURNE PARK, 1675-1750

These mince pies are not the sweet confections we're used to at Christmas. They have a degree of sweetness in them but were a way of making pies that were eaten as a savoury course. I'm offering you the original and an alternative version which is more like our modern one. There is, though, still a strong tradition of these kind of meat and dried fruit confections eaten on the Welsh border and known as Katt Pies at some of the fairs that mark the rural calendar. If you like a mixture of fruit and meat, like lamb and redcurrant or goose and apple, these may appeal to you in their original form as well as the more modern version.

ORIGINAL VERSION

INGREDIENTS

1¹/2 lb shortcrust pastry

¹/2 lb suet

1 lb minced beef or lamb

¹/2 lb Coxes apples, cored and chopped, but not peeled

1 lemon, grated and juiced

¹/2 teaspoon each, ground cloves and mace

2 tablespoons caster sugar

1 teaspoon salt

1 egg, beaten

MODERN VERSION

For a sweet version replace the mince meat with 1 lb of currants, sultanas and candied peel, mixed together. Then proceed as the above method

METHOD

Mix the apples with the meat (or fruit), lemon juice and rind, spices, sugar, salt and suet. Use the pastry to line the spaces in deep patty tins, fill firmly with the mixture, cover with a lid and brush with the beaten egg. Bake in a preheated, Gas Mark 7, 210 °C, 425 °F, oven for 25 to 30 minutes until browned and cooked through. The sweet version will need 5 minutes less baking. Serve the savoury pies hot, they are a great alternative to sausage rolls. The surplus mince can be stored in a jar in the fridge for up to a week.

TO MAKE MINCE PIEES

Take a pound off beefe suitt and 2 pound of meatte and shred itt small allso shreed 2 or 3 wardens or pipins which you please and the pill off a Lemon or oringe amongst the meatt season itt wiith cloves and mace and suger and a Little salt make itt nott two black with suitt when y[ou]r pies be allmost soaked putt in a Little Claritt and suger on all the sided off your pies and itt will soak into them and give them a very good tast -

Winter Cheese

MARSHAM FAMILY, WHORNES PLACE, 17TH-18TH CENTURY

This is a cheese made from winter milk, not as rich as the summer variety, therefore pressed and salted more and with cream added to it to enrich it. It's not meant to be a long keeping cheese, though in a fridge after 3 days pressing it will last very well for up to a fortnight. It comes from a tradition, of course, where the great houses had farms attached to them. The Marsham family would have had cattle kept on the Saltings running down to the Medway from their house at Whornes Place. To acquire enough milk to make cheese like this these days, is something of an enterprise. The quantity I have suggested therefore is really very much smaller and meant for pleasure rather than as a means of storing a precious raw material long before refrigeration. As equipment you will need a large china or glass bowl, a large colander with a piece of wood or tile which fits into it neatly, some scale weights and a couple of large pieces of cheesecloth to line the bowl. You will also need somewhere reasonably cool to do this.

INGREDIENTS

1 gallon full cream milk

1½ pints cream

1 tablespoon rennet

1 tablespoon salt

5 ozs double cream

METHOD

Warm the milk to blood heat and stir in the 1½ pints of cream. Add the tablespoon of rennet, stir it around and put it into a glass or china bowl. It will start to curdle and separate. Let it do this in its own time. After about 2 hours, when it has cooled and fully curdled, turn it gently using a tea plate to cut through the curds. Using the plate, scoop out the solid matter and put it into a colander lined with the cheesecloth. Put the piece of wood on it and add first ½ lb and then 1½ lb weights. Turn the cheese in the cloth and weight it again after about 4 hours. Leave it another 4 hours and then unwrap it from the cloth and cut it into thin slices. Rinse the original bowl and fill with fresh water. Place the slices of cheese in the water, strain them through the colander, tip them into the dry bowl again, crumble it with a potato masher or fork and stir in the extra 5 ozs of cream and the salt. Place it back in the colander in a clean cheesecloth, put the piece of wood or plate over the top and weight it with a ½ lb weight, adding another 1 lb each day for 3 successive days. Turn it every 24 hours. When firm remove from the colander, shape without removing from the cloth (a cake tin is good for this lined with greaseproof paper), and allow to mature for up to a fortnight before using. It tastes like a mild Caerphilly. It can be matured for up to 4 or 5 weeks but beware not to allow any green mould to develop.

Sack Posset

HUSSEY FAMILY, SCOTNEY CASTLE, 18TH CENTURY
MARSHAM FAMILY, WHORNES PLACE, 17TH-18TH CENTURY

Sack Posset was the winter warmer of the 16th, 17th and 18th centuries, a kind of hot Avocat or egg nogg, a drink that's still popular in Holland though it's fallen out of favour in Britain for some years. It's a very nourishing drink this, often taken late at night before going to bed. It's certainly very different from Horlicks. There's a prose and a poetry version in the collections and both are incredibly rich. I've amalgamated them in a slightly lighter version that can be served as an end of dinner treat as well as a good night drink.

INGREDIENTS

1½ pints Channel Island milk

1 blade of mace

6 size 3 eggs, beaten until frothy

1 teaspoon grated nutmeg

½ pint sweet Madeira or Oloroso sherry

3-4 ozs caster sugar

METHOD

Scald the milk bringing it to the boil with the mace and let it cool. Heat the sherry or Madeira in a saucepan with the sugar until the sugar has melted. Whisk the mixture whilst adding the nutmeg and the eggs. Strain the whole mixture into the milk and bring it gently to the boil until it thoroughly coats the spoon. Take it off the heat, cover and let it stand for at least 20 minutes in a warm place before serving in thick glasses.

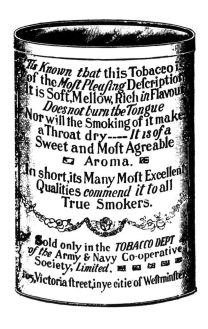

TO MAKE A GOOD SACK POSSET
Take - 2 - quarts of Cream or 2 quarts of New Milk - boil it with a blade of Mace & let it stand till it is Almost Cold while the milk is Cooling beat - Twelve Eggs - yolks & Whits & Grate in half a Nutmeg then put in a pint of Sack but if the sack be very Strong less will Serve - then sweeten it to your tast & when your Sugar is Melted Strain it into your Milk, & Set it over a gentle Fire keeping it Continually Stirring & when it is so thick that it hangs to the Spoon, take it off the Fire - & pour it as high as you Can into a Bason that it may froth, & Cover it & let it Stand half an hour and then Serve it up -

Punch

Punch was a great drink for hospitality in the 18th and 19th centuries. It was often made in advance rather like our Pimms type cups and used neat or diluted as the occasion required. Although they differ in quantity these recipes are really very similar in kind, being based on citrus juices and rum. A more refined punch would have been made with brandy instead of rum. Later in the century cold, china tea might also have been used to flavour and dilute the mixture.

This recipe may be diluted with lemonade or soda water when you come to drink it.

INGREDIENTS

(For 10-12 people)

6 pints of water

1 litre of rum or brandy

1 pint orange juice

½ pint lemon juice

12 ozs caster sugar

*Pared rind of 6 oranges
and 6 lemons*

METHOD

Place the peel in a jug with the sugar. Bring the water to the boil and pour it over. Stir thoroughly and allow to cool. Add the fruit juices. At this point it makes an excellent non-alcoholic punch. Add the rum, mix together and allow to stand. Strain into bottles or flasks.

FOR MAKING PUNCH
Mr Drummond

*First peel three lemons very thin, then put the peel into a large Jug with one pound of loaf sugar. Pour two quarts of boiling water in the Jug, & cover it over. Let it stand until quite cold. then add the juice of two Lemons, and half a pint of the best **Rum**: afterwards strain it, & it will be fit for use when **Iced**.*

PUNCH ROYAL
by Mr Apelin of Banbary 1779

One Gallon of Rum or Brandy, 2 Gallons of Water, one Quart of Orange Juice, one pint of Lemon juice, 6 Orange parings, 6 Lemon parings. Boil the Water, & sugar together. There must be 2 pounds of Loaf Sugar; & so in proportion to any Quantity. Put the punch in a Cask, till fit for Bottles, or Draught; But let it be as fine as Wine, before you bottle it.

*Punch Royal by Mr Apelin of Banbary 1779
One Gallon of Rum or Brandy, 2 Gallons of Water; one Quart of Orange Juice, one pint of Lemon juice, 6 Orange parings, 6 Lemon parings. Boyl the Water, & sugar, together. There must be 2 pounds of Loaf sugar. & so, in proportion to any Quantity. Put the punch in a Cask, till fit for Bottles, or Draught; But let it be as fine as Wine, before you bottle it.*

Index

Acknowledgements

The cover and title photographs and the photographs on pages 11, 15, 30, 47, 51, 58, 59, 87, 103, 107, 110, 118 and 134 were taken by kind permission of Viscount De L'Isle of Penshurst Place.

The photographs on pages 35, 39, 43, 66, 71, 82, 115 and 127 were taken by kind permission of Mr and Mrs John Warde of Squerryes Court.

Both Penshurst Place and Squerryes Court are open to the public.

The photographs on pages 42, 72, 105 and 132 are reproduced with kind permission from E J Sidery and were taken by William Henry Boyer.

Props by kind permission of Heals, Tottenham Court Road, London, W1.

Thanks to the Chevening Trust for the use of a number of jokes and quips from the two *Stanhope Commonplace Books*, 1848 - 1891.

Thanks to the Food and Agriculture Organisation of the United Nations for the two illustrations (the chubb mackerel and the oyster) from *Catalogue of Names of Fishes, Molluscs and Crustaceans of Commercial Importance in the Mediterranean*, FAO, 1965.

Additional illustrative material supplied from :
3,800 Early Advertising Cuts
Dover Publications,Inc.,

An Old-Fashioned Christmas
Dover Publications, Inc.,

A Facsimile of the Army and Navy Co-operative Society's 1907 issue of Rules of the Society and Price List of Articles sold at the stores
Army and Navy Co-operative Society,

Gustave Doré,

and the Centre for Kentish Studies.

Our grateful thanks go to the owners of the individual manuscripts who have given permission for the recipes to be used in this book.

The prints of the houses which appear in the book are as follows:
Page 23 Bradbourne Park
Page 36 River Hill
Page 64 Knole
Page 77 Chevening Place
Page 92 Penshurst Place
Page 97 Vinters
Page 114 Penshurst Place
Page 125 The Mote
Page 130 Chipstead Place